THE BABYLONIANS

D0368191

For centuries, Babylon has been a symbol of the decadent city *par excellence*, signifying a deep mistrust of urbanisation in general. In the Bible, the city has only negative connotations; and while later classical writers admired the city's size and splendour, they deplored some of its more unusual customs.

Whatever the perspective, it was usual to take Babylon as standing for the whole of Mesopotamian civilisation. The history of the Babylonians spans some 1800 years, from the time of Hammurabi, famous for his Law-Code, to the time when Alexander's heirs ruled the Near East. Archaeological discoveries and cuneiform tablets recovered from Babylonian cities allow us an impression of the Babylonian people and their society, their intellectual and spiritual preoccupations.

Gwendolyn Leick's approachable survey introduces these people, the reality behind the popular myth of Babylon. She explores the lives of kings and merchants, women and slaves, and the social, historical, geographical and cultural context in which their extraordinary civilisation flourished for so many centuries.

Enjoyable and accessible, this is the ideal introduction to the Babylonians for both students and the interested general reader.

Gwendolyn Leick is the author of several books on the ancient Near East, including *Who's Who in the Ancient Near East* (Routledge 2001), *A Dictionary of Ancient Near Eastern Mythology* (Routledge 1998), and *Mesopotamia: The Invention of the City* (2002).

THE BABYLONIANS

An Introduction

Gwendolyn Leick

London and New York

First published 2003
by Routledge
11 New Fetter Lane, London EC4P 4EE

Simultaneously published in the USA and Canada
by Routledge
29 West 35th Street, New York, NY 10001

Routledge is an imprint of the Taylor & Francis Group

© 2003 Gwendolyn Leick

Typeset in Garamond by
Florence Production Ltd, Stoodleigh, Devon
Printed and bound in the USA

British Library Cataloguing in Publication Data
A catalogue record for this book is available
from the British Library

Library of Congress Cataloging in Publication Data
A catalog record for this book has been requested

ISBN 0–415–25314–4 (hbk)
ISBN 0–415–25315–2 (pbk)

CONTENTS

FIGURES

INTRODUCTION

The city of Babylon was the most emblematic representation of Mesopotamian civilisation that the world remembered for centuries. In the Biblical accounts Babylon has only negative connotations, beginning with the account of the Tower of Babel in Genesis to the madness of Nebuchadnezzar and the death of Belshazzar in the book of Daniel. In the Revelations of St John the city even appears as 'Babylon the Great, the Mother of Harlots and Abominations', who 'corrupted the earth with her fornication'. The Biblical condemnation that decries the hubris of metropolitan degeneracy and the idolatry of its jewel-bedecked gods reflects an ideology which contrasted the purity of Israel's pastoralist past with the iniquities of urban life for which the exile was seen as a divine form of retribution. The urbane classical writers on the other hand, notably Herodotus, much admired the very size of the city and the splendour of its monuments while deploring some of the more bizarre customs, such as womenfolk prostituting themselves once a lifetime in the sacred precinct. Such accounts also emphasised the cultural distance between the morally superior Greeks and the inhabitants of the Orient under Persian control. Through the conquests of Alexander the Great the Hellenic world was briefly incorporated in an essentially Middle Eastern one; and according to some accounts he had plans for Babylon to become the capital of his new empire. Had this ever happened the city would have been anchored more firmly in the memory of the West. As it was, the Biblical negative associations prevailed and they also inspired Rastafarian references to 'Babylon' as the representation of any urban, Western and capitalist centre where black people suffer marginalisation and poverty.

1

More than any other ancient civilisation, including Rome, Babylon remains a symbol that expresses a deep-seated distrust of or at least ambiguity towards urbanisation. The confusion of tongues, architectural monumentality, the oppression of an under-class, the loosening of kinship ties and a fear of uncontrolled sexuality seduce and repel the more provincial cultures first confronted with the phenomenon. From the Babylonian point of view, the city was the most distinctive mark of their civilisation, a divinely decreed form of society which was never challenged.

The 'real' Babylon is slowly becoming more visible. The German excavations of the ruins around Hilla – some hundred kilometres south of Baghdad – which began in 1899, unearthed the foundations of vast palaces, temples and ceremonial streets. But in order to get an impression of Babylon's glory one has to travel to Berlin where the glazed portals of the famous Ishtar Gate have been re-created within the national museum. For the citizens of modern Baghdad the ancient Mesopotamian town is a popular destination at weekends. Under the auspices of the Iraqi Directorate of Antiquities and with the approval of Saddam Hussein, some of the old structures have been re-created with new bricks, giving the site a strangely contemporary outlook.

But the most precious evidence unearthed by archaeological excavations are the thousands of cuneiform tablets that were written by the 'real Babylonians'. Tablets have been found in quantity since the mid-nineteenth century and continue to emerge with almost every new dig. The few hundred Assyriologists around the world face the often arduous and frustrating task of categorising, copying, trans-lating and interpreting these texts which provide our main link to the long-vanished world of Mesopotamia. They allow us to reconstruct the development and history of Babylon and the various Babylonian states which the city controlled over the time-span of some one and a half thousand years. But while the political fortunes of Babylonia are of great interest in themselves, they also reveal social problems, intellectual obsessions and some of the minutiae of everyday living. This book aims to explore who the Babylonians were, what they con-tributed to the process of civilisation and what were their intellectual and spiritual preoccupations. To some extent the evidence is slanted, since the tablets reflect the attitudes and thinking of a literate elite. We know very little about the common people in the cities, let alone the tribal groups who populated the more marginal regions of the countryside. However, because literacy was so central to the effective management of Babylonian society, the legal and administrative records together with receipts of rations and lists of workmen give us some insight into working practices, restraints and possibilities for a cross-section of Babylonian citizens. Furthermore, archaeologists have begun to shift their attention from their original quest for monumental architecture to more mundane and humble dwellings and artefacts, and their findings provide valuable additional information about the quality of life in Babylon across the social strata.

I will first explore the geographical setting of Babylonia, the alluvial landscape between Tigris and Euphrates which had a profound effect on the socio-economic development of the region, and introduce the reader to local perceptions of space and the spatial order of the world which the cuneiform sources describe. This is followed by a discussion of literacy and the transmission of knowledge through the medium of cuneiform.

Chapter 2 deals with the history of the Babylonians within the framework of Mesopotamian history. Political dynamics, such as the tendency towards small city-state units and the formation of centralised states, as well as the immigration and absorption of tribal groups, had precedents in the time period before the Babylonians appeared on the historical stage. The emergence of competitive inter-state relations within the whole of the Middle East were a new development of the mid-second millennium, and the 'empire period' of the first millennium would have been unthinkable without the rise and fall of Assyria. The concept of Babylonia as a cultural unit within a Near Eastern context gradually developed. It cannot be understood in terms of a modern nation state with defined boundaries, a common language and a shared cultural identity. Ruling dynasties were sometimes of foreign origin, or the country was divided into more or less hostile territories, or under the political control of another state. The urban population of the ancient Mesopotamian cities had little in common with the tribal pastoralists in the periphery. The Babylonia of Nebuchadnezzar II was very different from that of Nebuchadnezzar I. The coherence of Babylonian history could be seen as largely illusory, as the result of an ideological system which anchored the regime of the day to an illustrious and ancient transmission of authority (the king lists). I therefore discuss the different periods as defined by linguistic distinctions rather than mere dynasties. This allows us to see continuities and changes which transcend the pigeon-hole divisions of the chronological system based on political control. The culmination of Babylonian learning happened when Babylonia had even ceased to exist as an independent state.

Chapter 3 explores the social and economic structure, paying particular attention to those institutions which were of primary importance to Babylonian society, such as the temple and the palace, as well as occupational groups within and beyond these institutions. The complex interrelationship between the 'private' and the collective within an urban setting was one of the most enduring characteristics of Mesopotamian civilisation.

Chapter 4 deals with the conceptual and spiritual world of Babylonian religion. Ritual practice and the power of the spoken and written word were harnessed to deal with all problematic aspects of human existence, misfortune and death, barrenness and defeat. Furthermore, the subject of the unpredictable became such a major intellectual challenge to result not only in the intricate lore of omens and divination but in the first scientific observation of stellar phenomena.

Finally, in Chapter 5, I present a brief survey of the material culture of the Babylonians – their dwellings and clothes, utensils and food – which characterises a people as much as their abstract ideas and social stratification.

This book is meant as an introduction and as such it skims the surface. There are some highly interesting subjects that I have not even superficially discussed – especially cuneiform mathematics which I never managed to get to grips with. The selection of topics reflects my own interests and preoccupations, and the perspective owes something to my other academic discipline, that of anthropology. I have attempted to write about the Babylonians in an ethnographic manner, picking up clues from the often random 'facts' recorded in tablets and derived from archaeological evidence. As all such descriptions it is selective and subjective since we often see only what we wish to see, and the interpretations of these 'facts' reflect the concerns and theoretical trends of our present time. Yet even a subjective experience will transmit some truths about a people and will hopefully entice the reader to continue exploring the world of the Babylonians in greater depth.

1

SETTING THE SCENE

GEOGRAPHY AND LANDSCAPE[1]

The dynamics of Mesopotamian history only make sense in view of the ecological and geographical conditions of the area. As the Greek name suggests, the lateral boundaries of the land known as Mesopotamia ('land between the rivers') more or less coincide with the main rivers, the western Euphrates and the eastern Tigris. The extensive marshland around the confluence of the rivers into the Persian Gulf forms a natural southern border. The northern frontier of greater Mesopotamia is constituted by the ridge of mountains which extends all along the south of the Anatolian plateau. Within this area there are two climatic zones: the northern part, known as Assyria, and Babylonia in the south. The main difference between them is the annual rainfall. The mountains to the north and east of Assyria ensure precipitation above a minimum of 200–300 mm per year, the amount necessary for a rain-fed agriculture. The rivers are wide apart and below the ranges of the Jebel Sinjar extends a semi-arid plateau known as the 'island' (*Jezirah* in Arabic) which could be utilised for seasonal herding of sheep and goats but was unsuitable for permanent settlements. This meant that the region was naturally divided between a western part, dominated by the Euphrates and its tributaries, and the eastern part along the Tigris and its side-arms from the mountains on the edge of the Iranian plateau. Culturally the Euphrates side was more closely associated with Greater Syria and orientated towards the Mediterranean, while the east looked towards Anatolia and Iran. The great Assyrian cities were all located in the east.

Figure 1.1 Assyria and Babylonia

In the south, rainfall is minimal due to the greater distance from any mountain ranges and the close proximity of the western desert. While most of the land in Assyria is formed by limestone and alluvial deposits, there is comparatively little stone in Babylonia, where the low gradient of rivers contributed to the thick deposit of alluvial sediment. Agricultural exploitation was possible only through irrigation but the alluvial soil was fertile enough to guarantee abundant and multiple crops (mainly of barley and emmer wheat). This potential for surplus of grain provided one of the most important incentives for population growth in the south. The stoneless earth also had the advantage that it was relatively easy to dig, which allowed for the construction of canals and subsidiary waterways. Thus the alluvial plains became a *tabula rasa* to be cultivated and populated at will. Villages and cities grew up along the rivers, as

6

well as between them, following the course of man-made or natural side-arms and canals which assured a year-round supply of water and provided the main means of communication (Fig. 1.2). The climate with its hot summers was also suitable for intensive date-palm cultivation, a highly important source of high energy food and timber. The country was less suited to herding, but owing to the economic importance attached to wool and the need for meat and dairy products, sheep, goats, pigs and cattle were kept on fallow land and on the agricultural periphery.

Geographically the southern plains were more isolated than Upper Mesopotamia. Along the eastern tributaries of the Karkeh and the Karun, contact with the Iranian lowlands was possible. Indeed, the region known as the Susiana had shared a common cultural development with Lower Mesopotamia since at least the sixth millennium. The western desert only proved less of a barrier once the camel had been domesticated in the late second millennium. However, because the southern alluvial plains were lacking in resources such as timber, minerals and stone, there was a strong incentive for trade. From the sixth millennium onwards such items were obtained from eastern Syria, Anatolia and the Iranian highlands.

Figure 1.2 The Tigris in southern Iraq (Photo H.D. Galter)

Visitors to Iraq find that most of the ancient cities of the south now lie in desert zones, amidst accumulations of sand. This is due to fluctuations of the river beds, as well as the gradual neglect of the old canal network between the main rivers in the early centuries of the Christian era. In antiquity the landscape of Babylonia was marked by intensive cultivation. Canals and ditches criss-crossed the plain, their sides elevated by frequent dredging. Date-palms, tamarisks and poplars were planted along the canals, and reeds edged the rivers and larger waterways. Villages were not a characteristic feature of the Babylonian countryside until the late second millennium and they are still poorly documented archaeologically. Cities rose from the level plains. Having been constantly rebuilt over millennia they could be seen from a long distance, with their mud-brick fortification walls and extra-mural suburbs at a lower level. At a distance from the cities and the cultivated land was the semi-desert (*ṣeru*) which was parched and empty in the hot months but verdant with new vegetation in spring. It was the habitat of semi-nomadic tribes who migrated with their flocks. In the very south, the 'Sealand', where the great rivers split into hundreds of side-arms, the landscape was dominated by extensive reed beds and inland lakes, a watery world where fugitives from the cities would hide among the tribal populations.

Although the rivers of Babylonia were the arteries of the land – bringing water and fertile sediments and serving as means of communication between cities – they were liable to change direction and shift their main course from one of the several beds to another. To some extent this could be controlled by the lateral canals, dams and diversion of waterways. Major shifts though, especially on the Euphrates, were beyond human interference and could cause the temporary abandonment of whole regions.

The climate also underwent periodic changes and there appear to have been prolonged periods of drought which lowered the water levels of the rivers and below ground. One such period which occurred around 1300 may have been partly responsible for the large-scale civic disruption throughout the ancient Near East although the ultimate causes, volcanic eruptions or other high-impact phenomena, are still unknown.

Geography was Mesopotamia's destiny in so far as the peculiar conditions of the region favoured a mode of living in densely populated urban centres in the alluvial plains and a more dispersed form of settlement further north. Mesopotamia always remained a primarily agricultural society and although the alluvial plains had a potentially phenomenal fertility, they had to be worked with care and restraint. The rich soil could provide surplus yields to feed a growing population but over-irrigation would result in washing salts to the surface and thus rendering fields unusable for several years. The political vicissitudes of the country often found their cause and effect in environmental degradation. While central control was vital to ensure the efficient maintenance of large-scale infra-structures, it could also lead to increased taxation and hence over-production. Again and again we see that strongly centralised states collapsed after decades of bad harvests when the carrying capacity of the land had been exhausted.

Mesopotamian civilisation was built on the intelligent manage-ment of the natural resources which, despite periodic setbacks, was maintained successfully for some 3000 years. When the knowl-edge and energy to sustain the waterways became lost, as happened sometime during the Parthian occupation of the land, the Babylonian world disappeared for ever.

BABYLONIAN GEOGRAPHICAL AND COSMIC NOTIONS

When we look at an ancient culture like that of Mesopotamia we import our contemporary vision and geographical parameters to locate it within a temporal and spatial grid which informs the modern view of time, the present knowledge of the world. The Babylonians had a very different outlook. In order to understand how they saw their world we need to examine their own documentation.

Anthropologists maintain that the making and reading of maps is a universal human activity, and quite independent of the use of writing.[2] It is striking that there are so very few cuneiform maps – some twelve geographical maps as opposed to the much larger num-ber of architectural and field plans[3] – although there are some designs on pottery from the preliterate Mesopotamian period which have been interpreted as having topographical referents.[4] It appears that the Babylonian scholars were more concerned with the names of places rather than their geographical relationship to each other. The visual conceptualisation became less important than the verbal one as knowledge became transmitted by writing. This process begins very early, almost as soon as writing was invented, in the mid-fourth millennium. There are archaic examples of lexical lists enumerating place-names and other toponyms which form the forerunners of the later, more standardised, geographical lists. The entries were arranged by order of graphemes or phonemes, and according to a long-established status-ranking which goes back to the third millennium BC.[5] In the standard Babylonian lexicon, known as *HAR.ra=hubullu*,[6] the geographical section begins with a list of fields, followed by cities,[7] regions and countries,[8] buildings,[9] mountains,[10] rivers,[11] canals, dikes and stars. While this work enjoyed wide circulation and was often copied in school tablets, it was by no means the only topographical list, since various other versions are known which follow a similar layout. The geographical data are arranged in a system which proceeds from the most fundamental constituent, the arable field, to the most distant, the stars of heaven. Fields are followed by cities, the basic political and social unit in Mesopotamia. The sequence of cities reflects traditional prestige rather than historical importance. Within the city section we find buildings and institutions associated with urban centres, such as palaces, temples and taverns. Thereafter the sequence varies. Some lists include here countries and regions, followed by mountains and rivers; others proceed to rivers and subsidiaries headed by the Tigris and Euphrates, man-made waterways and the marshes. Interestingly, the sea is omitted in most of the preserved texts. The mountainous regions in close proximity to Mesopotamia, such as the Zagros range and the foothills of Assyria, were called after the people who inhabited these regions, while more distant ones were associated with their main produce – hence the cedar mountains, the copper mountains, the silver mountains and so on. The names of regions inhabited by tribally organised groups occur only in some lists and preserve obsolete as well as current names but there is no section as such which would deal with foreign lands.

While we can clearly see that there is a genre-specific logic to the lists, with its graphic and oral referents, they nevertheless convey an image of how geographical space was conceived. It clearly reflects the perspective of an agrarian and urbanised society within the alluvial plains of Mesopotamia, a self-contained world centred on its cities and riverways. The list format was inherently conservative. Even the late Babylonian examples, written at a time when Babylonia was part of a multi-national empire, preserve a much older and to some extent anachronistic content based on scribal transmission. They maintain the geographical framework of the old, more parochial world of the third millennium with its city-states and ancient canals.[12]

Literacy references

Purely descriptive accounts of foreign places, such as those by classical writers, did not form a separate literary category in Mesopotamia. Royal inscriptions and epic narratives occasionally contain passages of often stereotyped accounts of exotic locales.[13] While Assyrian royal inscriptions are full of very detailed accounts of places conquered by their kings and where one can sense a relish in the reiteration of foreign place-names, Babylonian writers not only eschewed the reporting of military campaigns generally but also displayed a fundamental disinterest in their foreign dependencies. In Nebuchadnezzar's inscriptions there are only vague references to his rule 'over the inhabited world, from upper to the lower sea'. The literary texts, such as the Gilgamesh Epic, abound with descriptions of mythical and fantastic regions, such as 'Grove of Gem-bearing Stones' or the Mashu Mountains where the Scorpion people live, but the only real 'other' world depicted is that of the Mesopotamian semi-desert.

Of much greater interest to the Babylonians were more esoteric matters. They questioned as to how the universe was constituted, how the world began to take shape and what was the relationship between heaven and earth. The most important text about these things was the Creation Epic, known in Babylonian as *enuma elish*, literally 'when above', after its initial lines:

> When above heaven had not yet been named,
> when below earth had not yet been named.

It is a grandiose account which sets out from the unknown primeval chaos and proceeds to the detailed organisation of the Babylonian world on a cosmic pattern (Fig. 1.3). It is the god Marduk, offspring of the third generation of gods, the son of Ea, who takes on the task of creating the universe. He separates the primordially mingled waters into the sweet underground ocean and the salty sea. He then sets out the cosmic regions assigned to the gods Anu (the upper heaven), Enlil (the lower heaven and earth) and Ea (the subterranean region or Apsu), and arranges the position of the stars, sun and moon which provides the calendrical reckoning of time. He creates the sources of fresh water, rain and the rivers Tigris and Euphrates. The base material of creation is the anthropomorphic vast body of Tiamat, the female of the primordial pair of gods who had tried to stop the diversification of the universe. Man is made from the blood of a rebellious and slain god, imbued with divine breath, for the express purpose to relieve the gods from the labour of maintaining the world. Marduk rewards himself for his triumph with the creation of Babylon, 'the Home of the Great Gods' and his sanctuary. The poem concludes with the recitation of a hundred names.

The *enuma elish* establishes a correlation between the pre-eminence of Marduk and his city Babylon. It was recited during the New Year Festival when the statues of the main Mesopotamian gods travelled to the capital in order to confer sovereignty to Marduk and through him to the Babylonian king. Of great importance was the notion that Babylon is a link between the several vertical layers of the universe.

The earth was described as a disc-shaped piece of solid land that floats above the Waters of the Deep (Apsu) which well up as

Figure 1.3 Assyrian cylinder seal, c. 700 BC, which is thought to represent the battle of the god Marduk against Tiamat, as described in the Epic of Creation. (© British Museum)

groundwater or marshland.[14] The sky above is equally solid, like an inverted bowl, and subdivided into several celestial regions. The stars and the planets are attached to this firmament and travel in fixed routes across it. The lower world, including the underworld, where the dead dwell, and the Apsu are also dome-shaped, mirroring the world above. The notion that certain sacred spaces – originally Nippur, then Babylon – form a connection between the different cosmic layers had a long tradition in Mesopotamia. The Sumerian expression dur.an.ki 'the bond between heaven and earth' refers to the link between the earth and the upper regions, presided over by the great celestial gods. The names of some of the stepped pyramids, known as ziggurats, also reflect their function as a cosmic feature; the one in Babylon was called é.temen.an.ki 'House (of) the foundation of Heaven and Earth'. These structures were solid, containing no rooms inside. They were artificial mountains which allowed the officiating priests to ascend closer to the sphere of the deities.

The Babylonian cosmic geography projects the experience of inhabiting the alluvial plains into a universal scheme; the flatness of the earth where mountains are viewed as distant bulwarks retaining the boundaries of the world, the twin rivers and groundwater as the main sources of sweet water, a primordial substance like a sea which rings the earth and the vault of heaven suspended, like a bright kettle, above the earth. The cities, especially Babylon and Nippur, were not the result of human ingenuity but form part of the cosmic plan as primary links between heaven and earth.

Maps and plans

While the written sources concerning geographical and universal space are much more numerous, there are also some graphic representations, plans of buildings and fields on the one hand, and city maps on the other. The former were drawn up to give exact measurements of walls and boundaries and to indicate their placement.[15] It is likely that especially the temple plans were the result of surveys to establish the course of previous walls. Since the measurements alone contained the crucial information it was not necessary to draw to scale.[16] Babylonian temple building was inherently conservative and inscriptions often stress that not a single brick had been altered when a structure which had become dilapidated was reconstructed.

There are some very rare instances of elevations of ziggurats which concern vertical measurements and proportions but on the whole a building was adequately described by the placement of perimeter walls and major doorways. It appears though that the more sketchy plans were actually used as school exercises to solve mathematical problems, such as the calculation of areas.

The city maps – some twelve, more or less fragmentary examples are known – are schematic representations of certain features of the given city, especially water-courses, city walls, sanctuaries and main streets. Best preserved is the plan of Nippur which dates from c. 1500 (Fig. 1.4). This is drawn to scale and shows the city walls, the river Euphrates running straight through the city, with its major canals, the enclosure of the temple of Enlil, even store houses and a park.[17] The city walls were shown in great detail, complete with moats, and it has been suggested that the purpose

Figure 1.4 Plan of Nippur, c. 1500 BC. It shows the city wall with its seven gates, the Euphrates and two canals, as well as the enclosure of the Enlil temple (on the upper right-hand side). The names and some dimensions of all these features are indicated in the map. (18 × 21 cm) (Hilprecht Collection, Friedrich-Schiller Universität, Jena)

of the map was to facilitate repairs of the city's fortifications. None of the surviving city maps are oriented to the points of the compass; the Nippur map deviates by c. 45 degrees so that the top part corresponds to north-west.[18] Three further map fragments concern Nippur. Two depict the region outside the city, the first showing canals and a road, marked by a straight line that leads to a town, and the other refers to fields in relation to irrigation channels and small villages. The third concerns the city of Nippur again, but only a large building in the centre and a main road are preserved. Similar fragments also exist of Babylon, indicating the watercourses and the city gates. It is clear from all these examples that such maps represent existing boundaries and connections. They also emphasise the great importance of rivers and waterways in Babylonian spatial orientation since they connect and separate fields and villages, regions and cities. The boundaries of agricultural land, and exact data about the given surface, were also crucial to establish ownership rights and to plan agricultural investment and labour. Finally, the city walls not only defined the territorial boundaries but also formed a protective shield against hostile forces. The city wall epitomises the Babylonian city as much as the sanctuaries; their repair and maintenance was a royal responsibility.

While the architectural and field plans as well as the city maps reflect a built and geographical reality with considerable accuracy, in order to fulfil a practical purpose such as repairs and surveys, there is also a rather different map – accompanied by a written commentary – known as 'The Babylonian Map of the World' (Fig. 1.5).[19] The drawing on one side of the partially damaged tablet consists of a circle, identified as 'the bitter' (sea) surrounded by originally eight or seven triangular star shapes, called 'regions'. Within the circle are two parallel lines running from top to bottom, identified as the river Euphrates, as well as circles bearing the names of cities and districts, and two rectangular boxes called 'Babylon' and 'swamp'. A semicircular line at the top of the waterways is marked 'mountain'. This map does not attempt to draw either to scale or render exact geographical positions – Assyria is shown as south of Babylon and Susa due south, minor cities as well as whole regions are placed within the same-sized circles and there is also the significant absence of the river Tigris. However, the map, as all others, shows boundaries, here indicated by the circular parameter of the 'sea' – within

Figure 1.5 Babylonian 'Map of the World'. Sixth century BC. The rectangle above the hole in the middle represents the city of Babylon, the perpendicular parallel lines the Euphrates, and the circular band the ocean. (12.5 × 8 cm) (© British Museum)

it lies the world of Mesopotamia vertically shaped by the river Euphrates which begins in the 'mountains' and flows down to the marshes and swamps towards the 'lower sea'. On either side of the River are representative examples of the inhabited and familiar world which includes East Anatolian Urartu (subjugated by the Assyrians in the eighth century), the Iranian Susa, as well as tribal regions (Bit-Yakin, homeland of the Chaldean Dynasty, and Habban), Assyria, and Der. Babylon features prominently as straddling the Euphrates. Beyond the 'sea' are regions, of which one is described more fully as 'Great Wall, 6 leagues in between where the Sun is not seen'. The text on the reverse of the tablet is hard to understand, partly because of the bad state of preservation and partly because of its esoteric vocabulary. It refers to the eight 'districts' on the map and is phrased like a mathematical problem. For instance: 'to the third region, where you travel 7 leagues, a winged bird cannot safely complete its journey'. The written comments on the front, above the diagram, are equally obtuse, mentioning ruined cities as well as a number of animals (among them the viper, gazelle, panther, wolf, ostrich, chameleon and cat). They all have a connection with remote and unknown regions of the world. It is doubtful whether the map was meant to reflect a mere 'interest in distant areas' as Horowitz proposes. There is nothing to suggest that it refers in any way to the vast territories of the Assyrians for instance. Nor does it address any imperial political aspirations and achievements of the Neo-Babylonian empire which took over most of the Assyrian subject lands. The colophon at the end of the text reads:

[.....] . of the four edges of the entire.[...
[.....].: whose interior none one can kn[ow]
[.....] . copied from its old exemplar and collat[ed]
[.....] the son of Issuru [descend]and of Ea-bel-i{li}[20]

One could understand this as an admission that the far corners of the universe are fundamentally unknowable because they are well beyond even those areas which the heroic travellers of legend have reached, and that there is a 'back of beyond', which is immeasurable. It illustrates the contrast between what can be known, expressed by the scale of the Babylonian world, and what remains unfathomable. This resigned acceptance of the limitations of human understanding was a feature typical for some strands of Babylonian thinking which we also encounter in some of the 'wisdom literature'. Seen in this light the 'Babylonian Map of the World' does indeed document an interest in distant places, but as an epistemological challenge rather than as a distant forerunner to later world maps of conquering nations.

In conclusion the Babylonian texts and maps betray a pragmatic understanding of the configuration of their own world, with high value being placed on the antiquity of its main cities, the vital importance of riverways and the exact placement and surface of arable land. They also demonstrate a conceptual framework that was shaped by millennia of a scribal tradition which delights in the long reach of its own transmission and the speculation about hidden correspondences between heaven and earth, the secret measurements of a cosmic geography which remains tantalisingly obscure.

WRITING

While the particularities of the physical environment determined the socio-economic pattern of life Between the Rivers, the complexities involved in making it all work produced literacy. Literacy is one of the most defining characteristics of Mesopotamian civilisation. By the time the Babylonians first appear as a people, writing had been in use for at least two thousand years. It was not an instrument restricted to a clerical or political elite but one which affected every member of society. This does not imply that the majority of people were able to read and write themselves but that they were embedded in an administrative system which permeated society.

Writing had been invented in the fourth millennium to serve the bureaucratic needs of the Uruk culture which from a base in the southern plains expanded to a large network of distribution and exchange of agricultural and manufactured commodities.[21] The writing material was damp clay and the signs were first drawn with a pointed instrument. The archaic signs were composed of those representing numerical values for different items to be measured – grain, oil, beer, fields, and so on – and signs for tangible things, as well as professional and administrative designations for those persons or institutions responsible for transactions. The encoded

18

information did not represent a message in a particular linguistic idiom but a 'memo' which could be decoded rather than 'read'. This changed in the third millennium, when the archaic repertoire of signs was adopted to express the forms of speech of particular languages.[22] This was done mainly through the principle of homophony. In Sumerian the word 'house' was a monosyllabic word; Assyriologists assume that it was pronounced like the German 'e'. The same sound appeared in many other contexts, such as designated grammatical endings and as a syllable in longer words. Only the value 'house' could be drawn as a picture but this sign could be equally used for any occasion the phoneme 'e' had to be written. The meaning of signs was further enlarged by being assigned abstract semantic values, such as verbal notions. The sign for 'shepherd' could also stand for 'to shepherd', and the combination of 'head' with an arrow (or bowl?) near the throat: 'to eat'. Many other verbs and abstract nouns were rendered by newly invented signs. This type of writing is much more complicated to decipher and needed greater familiarity with the system acquired through lengthy training. It was full of logographic signs which had to be rendered into the correct grammatical form by the reader in his head. Special signs, so-called determinatives, placed before or after a word helped to elucidate the context – this was especially useful for personal or geographical names. However, the persistence of word signs (logographs) and the poor development of an orthography tailored to the phonetic needs of a particular language had the advantage that this mixed 'rebus type' writing could be adapted to other languages without too many difficulties. The word signs could be 'understood' and simply 'read' in another language, with 'phonetic complements' added to avoid confusion when necessary. Thus we find that cuneiform in the third millennium was used to render Sumerian, the west-Semitic languages Akkadian and Eblaite, as well as Elamite (spoken in south-west Iran). Later on the Hittites and the Hurrians were also to adopt cuneiform for their own, again very different, languages. The visual style of writing had changed too, perhaps as a result of a change in the direction a tablet was held; the curved lines, always difficult to draw on damp clay, were replaced by linear strokes and wedges produced by imprinting the edge of a sharpened reed into the soft surface. In later periods, the Babylonian cursive writing is instantly recognisable by its archaising features which distinguish it from the more formalised ductus of Assyrian writing (Fig. 1.6). At the beginning of the Old Babylonian period, Mesopotamia had a thousand-year-old tradition of writing in two main languages, Sumerian and Akkadian. Scribes were ideally trained in both, although Sumerian probably died out as a spoken language during the first quarter of the second millennium. The period of the greatest expansion of the Babylonian way of writing was during the mid-second millennium, when it became the language of international diplomacy. Although the courts of Egypt, Hatti and Mitanni employed scribes trained in Babylonian cuneiform, it remained there an elite preoccupation and neither replaced existing writing systems, such as hieroglyphics, nor did it become generally adopted in hitherto illiterate cultures.

Alphabetic systems, much quicker to master and better suited to express phonetic properties of individual languages, proved ultimately more successful.[23] Different forms had first been invented in western Syria around the beginning of the first millennium. Aramaic became the most widely used form of spoken and written communication in the multi-national and multi-ethnic empires of Assyria, Babylonia and especially of Achaemenid Persia.[24] However, as far as the Babylonians were concerned, it lacked the kudos of the ancient tradition of the more complex form of cuneiform writing and its associations of wisdom and superior knowledge. Cuneiform writing died out only when the last vestiges of Babylonian economic independence were repressed, sometime after the first century AD.

The greatest majority of cuneiform texts concern administrative matters. After all this was the primary purpose of writing, to record precisely the sort of information that the human brain finds difficult to memorise – for example, lists of commodities and personal names, endless numbers for all types of quantities. In fact, measuring and counting were the primary concerns of cuneiform literacy. Since the agricultural exploitation of the land was primarily organised by large institutional bodies (see Chap. 3), making use of a large labour force and dealing with all kinds of tools, equipment and products, the correct calculations and record-keeping were of vital importance. For example, not only did the right amount of seed corn have to be computed for a certain size of field, as well as the time that had to be allocated for the teams of ploughmen and draught animals, but also the rations and fodder for men and beasts; the expected

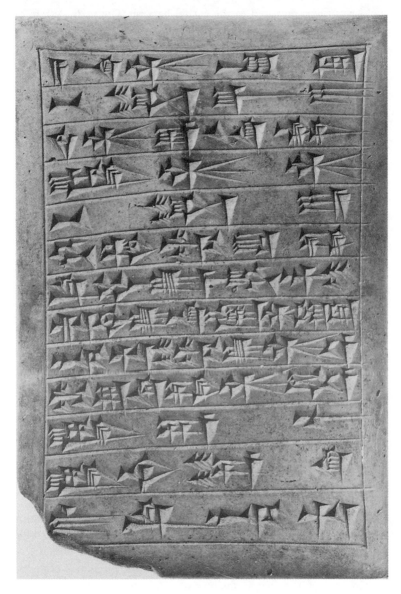

Figure 1.6 Cuneiform tablet. A Neo-Babylonian copy of a votive inscription of Hammurabi from c. 1750 BC. Hammurabi's name appears in line 7. The colophan specifies that the original was found in the temple Enamtila. (© British Museum)

yield was then compared to the actual harvest. The main system of counting was the sexagesimal system which had the advantage that it was the most suitable for the calculation of temporal units. The rendering of time was essential for the effective management of agricultural and all other civic tasks which had to be fitted into a seasonal cycle dictated by the local geophysical conditions. However, time was not seen as merely a convenient form of reckoning labour or leisure. More fundamentally, time was the divinely decreed rhythm of the universe – determined by the regular movement of the stars. All celestial phenomena, from the normal appearance and disappearance of the planets to irregular events such as lunar and solar eclipses, were thought to have a direct relevance to what happened on earth. The mathematical system echoes the perceived rhythm of the heavenly bodies which expressed itself in a coherent, predictable and numerically rigid way. This provided an ideal referent against which the deviations of reality had to be measured. There was also the question of how to reconcile several referents. The basic time intervals were the solar day, the lunar months and the solar year. The twelve lunar months make 354 days. This left a shortage of some twelve days for the solar year. The Babylonian solution was to adhere to the regular and ideal lunar 'year' but periodically, though irregularly, add a thirteenth, 'exceptional' month which was decreed by the king upon lengthy consultation by his diviners. This attitude of always assuming a regular measurement or blueprint against the intractability and irregularities of actual events was most characteristic for the Babylonian mentality. It had important repercussions for the way cuneiform mathematics and astronomy developed, but more generally this preoccupation with the discrepancy between the normative and the actual, which originated in the literate milieu, affected the whole society.

Cuneiform literacy provided an instrument of social control from which few people were ever exempt for long. It also, at least for the urban population, was a sign of Babylonian identity which was intimately linked to an intellectual tradition of thousands of years. It was one of the manifestations of 'wisdom' which was divine in origin. In the late period, when alphabetic scripts had become widespread, beautifully written cuneiform tablets were sometimes deposited as votive gifts for the gods, as the most suitable donation for the 'life' of a Babylonian.[25]

22

2

HISTORY

Babylonian history is embedded within a much longer sequence of Mesopotamian history. Modern scholarly chronologies differentiate a prehistorical period (from c. 6000–4000 BC), subdivided into epochs named after archaeologically significant locations, from a historical period (from 4000 BC to the beginning of the Christian era, or more commonly, the death of Alexander in 332 BC) which is defined by a succession of dynasties. Despite considerable problems in anchoring early dates to an 'absolute' chronological system, calibrating archaeological sequences with textual information and astronomical data such as eclipses, there is a generally utilised time scale which represents a form of compromise between the long chronology (now largely rejected) and the 'short' chronology still being hotly advocated by a number of historians. The resulting 'middle chronology' is the one adopted in those publications directed to a general readership.[1]

The overall structure of the chronological sequence is not a modern invention but derives from several Babylonian sources. Therefore our present view of Mesopotamian historical development rests fundamentally on an indigenous understanding and framing of history. The documents concerned are known as 'king lists'. The oldest one, the Sumerian King List, of which some twenty more or less complete copies survive, was compiled around 1800 BC by a Babylonian scholar. It begins with a section that lists eight kings who ruled for phenomenally lengthy periods of time, followed by the post-deluvian age 'after the flood had swept over (the land) and kingship descended from heaven (again)'. In the scheme of the Sumerian King List sovereignty was always exercised by one particular city at any one time and thus kingship passes from one Sumerian city to the next, beginning with Kish, then Uruk, Ur and Awan, then Uruk again, and so it goes on, sometimes for as long as the reign of a single king, sometimes for several. Thus the sequence continues until the lifetime of the author, at the end of the Isin dynasty. This prototypical list was later continued to comprise the time from the First Dynasty of Babylon (c. 1894–1595) to the reign of Nabopolassar (625–605) who founded the so-called Neo-Babylonian Dynasty; and the last one, the Seleucid King List, covers the Hellenistic period (from 330–125 BC). It has become clear that while the scheme worked as a consecutive sequence for the second and first millennia BC it was problematic for the third millennium when autonomous city-states coexisted side by side. The historical lists convey the Mesopotamian understanding of historical processes as unfolding in a linear time scale and a given geographical arena in which a number of cities are equal contenders for kingship. According to the Sumerian King List, kingship does not 'descend' on individual rulers but upon individual cities. In the later king lists, dynasties could also be named after the ethnic affiliation of the ruling elite (for instance, the Kassite or the Chaldean dynasty).

The chronological framework of Babylonian history, based as we have seen on the indigenous lists of succeeding dynasties, comprises the following scheme:

the First Dynasty of Babylon (from c. 1800 to c. 1600)
445 the Kassite Dynasty (c. 1600–1155)
the Second Dynasty of Isin (1155–1027)
the short-lived Second Dynasty of Sealand (1026–1006)
the Bazi Dynasty (1005–986)
330 the so-called Dynasty of E (976–647)
the Chaldean Dynasty (626–539).

Since the occupation of Babylonia by the Persian empire of the Achaemenids was not seen to constitute a major break with the religious and socio-political organisation of the country, the official end of Mesopotamian history has been taken to coincide with Alexander's defeat of Darius at Issos (333) which led to the incorporation of the 'East' into a 'Hellenic' world, dominated in western

Asia by the Dynasty of the Selucids. This particular date owes more to the Orientalist orientation of European scholarship, which regarded Greece as essentially 'occidental', than to a real and abrupt end of Babylonian civilisation.

There is also another, more broadly formulated chronological framework, based on linguistic changes in the way Akkadian was written. Hence Old Babylonian texts begin with the introduction of Akkadian as an official idiom of communication following the collapse of the UrIII dynasty in about 2000 until 1600. This phase is often regarded as the classic age of Babylonian writing. During the subsequent period ('Middle Babylonian', from 1600 to 1000) case endings are no longer clearly differentiated, and various phonetic changes occurred. However, in literary works, such as hymns and epics, a more archaic form of language was maintained. The language of the Neo-Babylonian phase (1000–600) was influenced by Aramaic which became even more strongly pronounced during the final period ('Late Babylonian', from 600 to the end of cuneiform writing in the first century AD). This frame of reference is quite widely used by Assyriologists whose major sources are textual. Archaeologists may prefer the 'three age system'[2] in which case the period from 2100 to 1600 could be classified as Middle Bronze, 1600–1500 as Late Bronze, and the Iron Age as beginning around 1200.[3] However, because of the abstract nature of this scheme, it does little to elucidate Babylonian historical or cultural development. In the following discussion I favour the broader division into Old, Middle and Late Babylonia for a general framework within which the various, sometimes short-lived, dynastic periods can be located.

MESOPOTAMIA IN THE THIRD MILLENNIUM

The most astonishing development of the late fourth millennium was the emergence of the first urban conglomeration, the city of Uruk in the southern plains of Mesopotamia. Uruk was the nexus of a massive network of exchange and distribution which included the Susiana as well as north-west Iran, Upper Mesopotamia and eastern Syria, right up to the mountains of Anatolia. Towns with identical architectural installations (large rectangular buildings and store-houses) and material culture have been found in all these regions and testify to a remarkable degree of cultural homogeneity. To what extent Uruk, by far the biggest city, also exercised political control over this large region is still hotly debated.[4]

By the beginning of the third millennium the situation changed, many of the 'Uruk' towns became abandoned and there is a marked disruption in the archaeological sequence in Uruk itself. The transitional Djemdet-Nasr period is followed by the Early Dynastic period (from c. 2600 to 2350). The first historical documents appeared, as well as a number of individual and self-contained polities, known as city-states. These urban centres developed along the main waterways – and increasingly along subsidiary branches and canals – and controlled a more or less strictly defined agricultural hinterland. Independent villages and smaller towns disappeared as the population became increasingly concentrated within walled cities. By the end of the third millennium the majority of the population lived in such cities which ideally functioned as clearly separate units, in competition with each other, or forming mutually supportive alliances. Competition between cities, especially over water rights, became intense and there was at times aggressive expansionism at the expense of weaker rivals, fanned by political leaders whose power was based on military success and control over agricultural resources. According to the surviving written records, each ruler vaunted himself as a rightful leader by virtue of divine favour – as one chosen by the gods. Attacks on other cities were presented as the will of city gods and goddesses who settled scores amongst each other. This pattern of inter-city rivalry was temporarily brought to an end by Sargon of Akkade (c. 2340–2284) who founded the first centralised state in Mesopotamia. Although other local rulers before him had managed to subdue and control a range of southern Mesopotamian cities for varying periods of time, no one had yet achieved a similar measure of centralisation and subjugation of local polities. His inscriptions also boast of foreign conquests, perhaps not more than aggressive sorties beyond the Mesopotamian plains, into western Iran and along the Euphrates into Syria, which did not establish any really long-lasting domination over such regions, but served to co-ordinate long-distance trade and certainly brought in revenue through tribute and prestations from further afield.[5] Sargon's two sons and grandson succeeded him as 'king of the four corners of the universe', a new title which underlined the hegemonic claims of the dynasty which was to last from 2350 to 2150. The capital of Sargon's kingdom, Akkad, was apparently a new foundation. To this day its exact location has not been archaeologically identified, but the city was situated in the north, perhaps in the area around present-day Baghdad. The Akkad kings were keen to achieve recognition from the older urban centres by making lavish gifts to temples. However, the reorganisation of taxes and the redistribution of land-holdings and trade revenue for the benefit of a central government were seen to contradict the interests of the old established, and hitherto independent, city-states. The Akkad government tried to overcome this resistance against a unified state by investing in the symbolically powerful religious institutions, by improving infrastructure and communications between cities, and by regular military campaigns against neighbouring territories. However, such stratagems worked only when the foreign wars resulted in victory, booty and tribute, when trade flourished and resources were plentiful. As soon as any setbacks occurred, or at the death of the old king, the separatist tendencies asserted themselves and the old cities attempted to regain their independence, sometimes by supporting external conflicts quite openly. In the royal inscriptions such moves are invariably couched as rebellions which had to be suppressed and punished. Such more or less brutal retribution stimulated further resentment and at the next opportunity hostilities against the ruling dynasty were renewed.[6] In the end it became unviable to unite the country by force and the 'empire' shrank to a small territory around the 'capital' which fulfilled this function but in name. Furthermore, the capital became vulnerable as a target of internal and external aggression, as a treasure trove of stolen bounty. Later, Mesopotamian historians were to blame the Gutians, a people originating from the Zagros Mountains at the Iranian border, for having destroyed Akkad, and the Sumerian King List duly credits the Gutians as the successors of the Akkadian dynasty. However, in the Mesopotamian south, the old pattern of independent or interdependent city-states reasserted itself. Particularly well documented is the city-state of Lagash, which prospered economically and even mounted successful attacks against Elam. Sometime in the 22nd century, a ruler of Uruk attacked the power base of the Gutians and, by the capture of their king, brought the 'foreign' dynasty to an end. Although the real extent of Gutian influence over Mesopotamia was most likely restricted to the north, and did by no means entail a massive occupation by 'barbarous hordes' or a repressive regime which held sway over the whole country, the overthrow of the Gutian ruler was subsequently portrayed as the harbinger of a new era and as a 'national' liberation. Such a view served the interests of a new centralised state which unlike the Akkadian state arose from within the Mesopotamian south, from Ur, the seat of the moon god Nannar-Suen. This dynasty, known as the Third Dynasty of Ur,[7] lasted for some 150 years, roughly up to 2000 BC. The kings of Ur, most notably its longest-reigning monarch, Shulgi (2094–2047), created a new centralised state which controlled all the Sumerian cities, as well as regions further north, around the late Akkadian rump state. Ur enjoyed great prestige as an ancient religious centre and the kings of the Third Dynasty emphasised their close links to the old Sumerian gods. The cultural heritage of Sumer was revitalised to enhance the legitimacy of the centralising state. Bilingual inscriptions disappear and the Sumerian written form had to be used for all administrative and legal procedures. We should be wary of interpreting this as a manifestation of ethnicity – it appears from the personal names people had at this time that there was no distinction between 'Sumerians' and Semites or indeed people speaking yet other languages. The insistence of privileging Sumerian as the only official (written) language serves to emphasise the state's respect for tradition and cultural continuity.[8] It was one of the many forms of ideological justification which much surpassed the efforts of Akkad. The measures of centralisation and bureaucratic control which the Ur state exercised were in fact unprecedented. The king's representatives governed all city councils, his men were elected to the most senior positions in the temple organisations, and the army and legislative were equally controlled from the centre. Production of textiles, one of the major Mesopotamian industries, was largely controlled by the palace, as was the import and export of various commodities and much of agricultural production. The system of taxation was made more comprehensive and efficient, and included hitherto exempt institutions such as important cult centres. However, it was equally in the king's gift to grant individual exemptions and privileges to ensure active support of ideologically sensitive organisations. Costly public festivals and displays of royal benevolence and respect for tradition and religion were regular features of the Ur kings' attempts to convince the population of their right to rule. However, as in the time of the Akkad state, all went well as long as extortion and investment were relatively balanced. When in due course the rising urban populations could no longer be adequately fed because of an overuse of agricultural land, and when pressures on ever higher levels of production became unsustainable, the hold of central government became precarious once more. Again, external causes were made responsible; this time it was 'barbarians' from the west, Amorite tribes people, who were said to threaten the stability of the state. Even modern histories keep repeating the same old ideological line of argument that it was the increased pressure of displaced nomadic tribes which brought the Ur state to its collapse. There certainly was an influx of western tribes into Middle and Lower Mesopotamia, but this was facilitated by a weakened economy, fields going to waste because of over-salinity and the abandonment of waterways because of neglected maintenance. In Mesopotamia the balance between population expansion and productivity was inherently problematic. Relatively smaller units of responsibility and control were better suited to react to ecological stress. The walled enclosure of the urban centre served to some extent as an impediment to population expansion. Furthermore, the maintenance of waterways, dykes and the fields through crop rotation and the fallow principles would work more efficiently when it served the resident population. Centralisation not only took away local control and responsibility but could also enforce rising production rates which accelerated the degradation of the ecological system in a whole area. One of the possible responses to falling productivity and the threat of famine was to increase transhumance livestock production. Eventually the Ur government was faced with widespread revolts from the old cities, as well as rising immigration by tribal groups. One king, Amar-Suen, even built a 170-mile-long wall to keep them out. The end of Ur is well documented by a series of letters exchanged between the last king of Ur, Ibbi-Sin (c. 2026–2004), and one of his senior officials, Ishbi-Erra, a man who had gained much influence in Middle Babylonia where he had been governor of Mari. When Ur was at the brink of starvation, Ishbi-Erra delayed the required shipments of grain for political reasons. He allied himself with some of the stronger opposition, formally joined other enemies of the Ur king, and took control over the remnants of the UrIII empire. He founded a new dynasty at Isin which was to last until c. 1850. Ur, the former capital, was destroyed and brutally sacked by the Elamites in 2007.

THE OLD BABYLONIAN PERIOD
(c. 2000–1600 BC)

The break-up of the UrIII state around 2000 can be taken as the point of departure for a new manifestation of Mesopotamian culture, largely determined by a strong Amorite influence. We have seen that peoples speaking West-Semitic languages had been part of the population of Mesopotamia since written records began in the early third millennium.[9] There was also a steady and sometimes markedly increased influx of tribally organised peoples from the Syrian desert regions who since the latter part of the third millennium were referred to as Amorites, a word which generally denoted the west. Shu-Sin, the last king of Ur, built a wall across the northern frontier of his kingdom (c. 2034) to keep them out but this proved useless and as soon as he was dethroned and the centralised government collapsed, Amorite sheikhs established themselves as rulers of existing city-states or formed new petty kingdoms. Mesopotamia thus reverted to the pattern of particularism, with a large number of small and medium-sized polities, especially in the northern part of the country. The situation in the south was somewhat different because Ishbi-Erra had assumed control over the core of the defunct UrIII state. He operated from the city of Isin which became the new capital and established the 'First Dynasty of Isin' in c. 2017. Ishbi-Erra was at pains to emphasise the continuity with the ideological premises of the previous regime, much facilitated by the fact that the old centres of religious importance (Uruk and Nippur) remained within his control – and maintained the cult of the UrIII kings. The Isin state operated in essentially similar ways to the previous one, exerting taxes from agriculture and deriving its main income from the lucrative international trade in luxury items via the Persian Gulf. However, the problems which had contributed to the decline of the Ur state had not vanished: the land suffered from overproduction, and the supply of water became an increasingly pressing concern for the south. This made it imperative to invest heavily in hydraulic projects, especially the building of new canals. Furthermore, the supremacy of Isin – which lasted for some 200 years – was persistently challenged by other city-states, especially by its southern rival, Larsa. The two cities began a protracted and bloody struggle for supremacy, cutting off each other's water supply and thus further weakening the ecological balance of the land. Larsa gained a temporary advantage by digging a major new canal and gaining control over the Gulf ports. The year 1794 spelled the end of Isin's dynasty, when Rim-Sin, the exceptionally able and determined king of Larsa, conquered Isin, which left him in sole control over southern Babylonia. This monarch, who ruled an astonishing sixty years (1822–1763), was also responsible for wide-reaching administrative and legal reforms. In summary we can say that during the first quarter of the second millennium, southern Mesopotamia continued to operate along the lines of the UrIII state both in terms of legitimising its authority through the theological support of the old cult centres of Ur, Uruk and Nippur, and by maintaining control over the seaborne trade via the Gulf. At the same time, the difficult ecological situation and the almost constant warfare between Isin and Larsa progressively weakened the subsistence basis of the land and caused civil unrest.

Let us now look at the north, where we saw a significant presence of Amorite groups, both pastoralists and agriculturalists. The northern plains and valleys were put to more intensive use through irrigation programmes along the main riverways. Pastoralist herding also increased proportionally as herders interacted with village and urban communities. These developments allowed for an expansion of the population and this had a profound effect on the political influence of the north to the detriment of the old southern cities.

A major force in the acculturation of the northern plains at this time were the Amorites and it comes as no surprise to find Amorite chiefs asserting their control over the whole of northern Mesopotamia.[10] This was divided into different spheres of influence, one centre of gravity being the eastern Syrian region, from Halab (modern Aleppo) to the Euphrates valley, the other around Mari along the middle Euphrates, extending further east to another centre around Eshnunna at the Diyala river, and another further north along the Tigris, the heartland of Assyria around Ashur. Last but not least there was Babylon on the Euphrates, right in the middle between Upper and Lower Mesopotamia. Babylon had not been an independent city, but it was a seat of provincial administration during the UrIII period. Since c. 1894, when an Amorite called Sumu-abum conquered the city, it functioned as a petty kingdom.

A further political player in the region was Elam in south-west Iran. The Lower Mesopotamian plains and the Susiana are geologically very similar and there are no natural obstacles between the two. As a result the two areas have had a more or less shared cultural development since the earliest phases of human occupation. In the third millennium when Mesopotamia became increasingly under influence from the west, owing to subsequent waves of immigration by Semitic tribes, south-west Iran received immigrants from the east. The first people who became historically evident, although it is not clear whether they were indigenous or not, were called Elamites, a name derived from the word *haltami* which was rendered as *elam* in Akkadian. The Elamite language is unrelated to any other known language. Having shared the same cultural development as southern Mesopotamia, urbanism and writing appeared at the same time and the Elamite also used a cuneiform system of writing. With the emergence of centralised states in Mesopotamia Elam began to become a potential target for raids and subjugation to tribute payment. The kings of Akkad and of UrIII led campaigns to this effect and thus claimed sovereignty over Elam. In time Elam retaliated and, as we have seen, Ur was in fact destroyed by the Elamites. Subsequently, under the so-called Sukkalmah dynasty (1900–1600), Elam became one of the largest and most powerful states in the area and exerted a great influence on the political situation in Mesopotamia.

We have seen that the political vacuum which arose from the breakdown of the UrIII state was filled by intense rivalries among a number of key players – Isin and Larsa in the south, Elam in the east, and the various Amorite kingdoms and sheikhdoms in the north and north-west. While the larger parties were more or less evenly matched in the number of warriors they could equip and maintain, smaller polities were forced to offer allegiance to whoever happened to assert their authority over them at any one point. Thanks to the archives of the city of Mari we are unusually well informed about the historical events of this time. Since it was of vital importance for local rulers to remain abreast of the ever-changing political developments, they maintained spies in the major urban centres as well as amongst tribal confederacies. These intelligence officers sent written reports to their master, often on a daily basis, which allowed leaders to react quickly to any new development. The Mari documents concern just the one city during the time of less than two generations. However, because of the close involvement of all Mesopotamian (and Elamite) parties, they present a much broader picture than just the perspective of a Middle Euphrates city-state. Furthermore, many of the rulers involved were tied to each other either by kinship relations – Shamshi-Addu placed his sons as governors of conquered cities for instance – or by diplomatic marriages. In fact, the Mari letters make it quite clear that daughters were meant not only to secure and symbolise politically expedient marriages but to spy on their husbands and their activities. A superior intelligence system was thus one of the main keys to political success. However, in the rapidly changing political climate, the most tenacious leaders also needed particular character traits in order to stay in the game. They had to be quick-witted, decisive, patient, obdurate and charismatic, dissimulating and ruthless. A tough physique and a talent for military strategy also helped. Most important was an ability to communicate with all the different social groupings and find the right tone to address both pastoralist tribesmen and urban bureaucrats. As the Mari archives demonstrate, leaders such as Shamshi-Addu fitted this description very well. Rim-Sin of Larsa was another long-lasting and highly able king and by the time he had gained control over the south by his capture of Isin, his power was unrivalled in Lower Mesopotamia. However, his hegemony proved short-lived when he was in turn eclipsed by a king of Babylon, named Hammurabi.

Hammurabi (c. 1792–1750) was the sixth king of an Amorite dynasty founded by Sumu-abum (Fig. 2.1). By the time he acceded to the throne of Babylon, his kingdom comprised a relatively small territory, that is the city of Babylon itself as well as the old urban centres Kish, Sippar and Borsippa. Sippar was the most important, a flourishing trading centre with two major sanctuaries including

Figure 2.1 Fragment of a stone slab inscribed with a prayer for king Hammurabi of Babylon, probably represented here with his right hand raised in a gesture of worship. (© British Museum)

the temple of the sun-god Shamash which the Babylonian kings endowed generously in an effort to make it more prestigious than the southern sun sanctuary at Larsa. Hammurabi's territory was in the geographical middle of Mesopotamia; halfway between Rim-Sin's capital in the south and Shamshi-Addu's seat at Ashur. Perhaps his most outstanding qualities were his patience and an ability to seize the right moment for action. At the beginning of his career he had to acknowledge the authority of Shamshi-Addu and Rim-Sin and joined in their military campaigns. At home he concentrated on improving the economic basis of his kingdom by building canals and strengthening fortifications. The situation changed after Shamshi-Addu's death in 1781 since neither of his sons proved to be as wily and tough as their father. Mari regained its independence under Zimri-Lim and Hammurabi allied himself with Mari in an effort to ward off danger from Elam which was also poised to make gains from Shamshi-Addu's demise. Then, after nearly thirty years, one success followed another in quick succession. Hammurabi finally defeated an eastern coalition led by Elam in his twenty-ninth year and secured control over the East Tigris region. Three years later he attacked Larsa, ostensibly because Rim-Sin had refused to join in the war against Elam. He captured the city after a six-month siege, took Rim-Sin and his son prisoner, demolished the fortifications but spared inhabitants and buildings. This victory signalled the annexation of all the old urban centres, such as Ur, Uruk, Isin and Larsa. The defeat of the old Assyrian stronghold Eshnunna gave access to the eastern trade routes across the Zagros Mountains. Two years later he turned against his former ally Mari and systematically destroyed the city by fire. He was now the undisputed ruler over the whole of Mesopotamia. Only the western kingdom of Yamhad, ruled from Aleppo, remained as a major rival power. He commanded over an empire of a similar size as that of UrIII, with all the major cult centres, and control over all the trade routes, from north to south and east to west. One of the most pressing concerns was the reclaiming of large parts of the country which had suffered from warfare, tribal unrest and flooding because of neglected waterways. Refugees from particularly devastated areas had to be resettled and provided for. Among them were also intellectuals and priests from the defeated and depopulated cities of the south, such as Isin, Larsa and Uruk. They were accommodated in the capital or neighbouring cities and allowed to build temples to their own deities.

Hammurabi also seems to have made use of the administrative reforms introduced by Rim-Sin and strengthened the state's powers of taxation. He was aware of the importance of securing the support of the religious and intellectual elite based in the old cities of the south. He invested heavily in the repairs and maintenance of temples, and encouraged scribal centres. The archives of Sippar and Larsa both show that the king was at pains to show himself accessible to his people and to embody justice. Numerous letters have survived which preserve the regular correspondence between the king and his senior officials, as well as letters and petitions by ordinary individuals who made complaints or requests directly to their ruler. The famous Law Code, engraved on a stone stele, also dates from this last period of Hammurabi's reign. Of particular interest are the lengthy prologue and epilogue which frame the legal pronouncements. Written in a highly poetic language, using an archaising script which imitates the royal inscriptions of the Akkadian kings, this text can be seen as a charter of Babylonian kingship. The text owes much to the phraseology of older royal inscriptions which had been assiduously copied in the scribal centres for centuries. The king is portrayed as having been chosen and called by the gods of the land and given dominion 'over the black headed people' – which means the whole of the population. His rule is therefore legitimised by divine forces. In Hammurabi's Code the Babylonian god Marduk, a previously little-known deity, now confers kingship along with Enlil and the other great gods of the country. Of great importance here is also the notion of the 'shepherdship'; the king and his people are shown to be in a relationship of shepherd and flock.[11] Like a shepherd he maintains internal order and defends his charges from predators but the metaphor also implies that the shepherd is the keeper not the owner of the flock. It is a responsibility also echoed in other phrases of the inscription which emphasises the stewardship bestowed by the gods. This contrasts with the Ur ideology where kings were seen to partake of divinity themselves. Another crucial aspect which had less currency in previous epochs was the stress on justice and righteousness towards all subjects. Unlike other rulers of his time, Hammurabi publicised his pursuit of justice in several year names which customarily recorded significant events of a given regnal year. The Law Code (publicised in his 39th regnal year) represents an attempt to formalise certain legal relationships and sets down tariffs for a number of commodities and fines. Careful attention is given to the duties and rights of people who were granted land by the crown in return for services. It also contains prescriptive legislation about a wide number of issues, from homicide to inheritance, accusations of witchcraft, damage to property, marriage and adultery, as well as professional conduct. It is notable that in comparison with earlier collections of legal precepts, where monetary fines were the norm, Hammurabi's Code stresses the talionic principle – 'the eye for an eye' rule. There is as yet only scant evidence to what extent the Code was followed in legal practice and some of the commodity prices were certainly idealistic rather than a reflection of reality. However, it documents one of the major concerns of Old Babylonian kingship: to obtain and maintain justice in the land. It is not known where the stele originally stood; some scholars think that it was put in a temple next to a statue of Hammurabi as 'king of justice' – to which reference is made in a text of the period. Even had it stood in a public place, only the most learned of scholars would have been able to read the highly archaic script. Several centuries later it was carted off to Susa by an Elamite king who had a foible for ancient monuments. It was there that French archaeologists discovered it in 1902 and it has been exhibited at the Louvre ever since.

Hammurabi's reign is often described as the high point of the Old Babylonian period. He unified the country into a single, centralised state which reached nearly the same dimensions as the UrIII empire. The forceful personality of the king is relatively well known because of the quite extensive correspondence that has survived. However, the 'empire' he had so skilfully and tenaciously acquired proved to be short-lived. One by one the subject regions asserted their independence; the middle Euphrates region was lost to a new Amorite kingdom based around Terqa, and the south – with the valuable access to the sea, its date-palm plantations and protein-rich marshes – was controlled by another new force which was later to be known as the Sealand Dynasty. Babylonia comprised thus its original territory in the centre of Mesopotamia as well as some of the old urban centres in the south. A new, if tenuous, equilibrium was the result of the shift in political boundaries which lessened the fierce competition of the first two hundred years. The main Amorite kingdoms were now the already powerful Yamhad and Hana. The kings of Babylon were ever more closely tied to the tradition of Mesopotamian heritage. Hammurabi's successors were keen to support the scribal centres of Nippur, Sippar and Larsa, and to establish new schools at Babylon. They rebuilt the sanctuaries of old cities as well as founding new shrines to the Babylonian 'national' deity Marduk. Above all they were keen to fulfil their roles as arbiters of justice, and one of the most important documents of the period is the *mešarum* act of Ammisaduqa which proclaimed freedom from debt obligations.

The dominant pattern of social life in the alluvial plains of Mesopotamia in the third millennium had been urban. Already by the Early Dynastic period nine-tenths of the population lived in settlements larger than 30 hectares with only very few villages.[12] Smaller settlements existed beyond the city walls but they were not independent. Mesopotamian cities were based on a rural economy which was organised from within the city rather than supported by the 'countryside'. Another factor was security. City walls and a higher number of people provided greater safety than unprotected village communities. In times of inter-city warfare and tribal raids, cities were safer. By the time of the UrIII empire the water supply had become precarious and the state had to invest heavily in providing new canals and a whole series of facilities such as weirs, locks and water reservoirs, as well as the organisation and man-power to maintain and oversee that all these installations worked efficiently. It appears that smaller towns began to proliferate perhaps in response to the new hydraulic projects. The increased presence of tribal Amorites by the end of the third millennium brought new pressure on the rural areas in the north and people began to gravitate towards better-protected large cities. In the Old Babylonian period, some areas were more heavily populated than others; we have seen that the centre shifted northwards, away from the low-lying southern plains with their particular problems with drainage and towards the region around Babylon and the north Meso-potamian plains.[13] This allowed a more mixed form of settlements, with more small and medium-sized towns, smaller villages and various 'camps' used by semi-nomadic groups. It is clear from the administrative documents of the period that villages flourished and although they were politically dependent on the local city they undertook the administration of their territory. It has been pointed out that in fact 'one hears more of the smaller rural settlements acting as an official body than we do of cities'.[14] Elders and the mayor represented the community and they were responsible for the jurisdiction in their area, the organisation of water rights, the observation of the fallow and so on. A similar pattern was reproduced in the cities, where separate 'neighbourhoods' known as *babtum* were also under the authority of elders and a mayor (Babylonian *rabianum*). To what extent such neighbourhoods were composed mainly of kinship groups no doubt depended on both the area of the city and the particular circumstances; however, it is clear that kinship clusters were a very common form of residence throughout Mesopotamian history and indeed even now in the present-day Middle East.[15]

Land was usually owned by the partilinear kin group and could be alienated only with the consent of all male members. A considerable proportion of land was thus owned privately, in addition to the substantial land-holdings of the large institutions, such as temples and the crown (see Chap. 3). It appears to be an innovation of the Old Babylonian period to lease certain tracts of mainly newly cultivated land, especially in conquered territories or hitherto marginal regions, to individuals in exchange for regular services, such as military duties, building of public works, canals and so on. While the UrIII state had maintained a monopoly on certain forms of manufacture, especially on textile production, the political fragmentation of most of the Old Babylonian period (excepting the relatively brief time of Hammurabi's 'empire') allowed greater economic liberalism. This was also very noticeable in trade where private enterprise was responsible both for the capital investment and the actual organisation of how and what goods were transported. This is particularly well documented for the nineteenth-century trade activities at Ashur and eighteenth-century Sippar. Metals – especially tin, bronze and silver – were imported from Anatolia and the Iranian highland, while craft articles, such as jewellery and especially textiles, both as cloth and as fully worked garments, were exported. The texts show that such trade was highly lucrative but that it could function only in politically stable times.

The Code of Hammurabi refers to three different types of legal persons: there are slaves, who are legally not persons at all but property – their owners had to be compensated accordingly for the loss; then there were 'men' (and 'women', *awilum* and *aššatum*) who had full legal rights to acquire and dispose of property. In addition the Code makes provisions for people called *muškenum* whose rights were restricted but who were not unfree. It is not clear how such a status was conferred and references to this term are rare outside the Code. The term was not used during subsequent periods. Perhaps the *muškenum* were tied to the palace in some form of obligation but the problem is far from clear.

The archives of Larsa, which date mainly from Hammurabi's last ten years, show how closely the king was personally involved in

local affairs. He insisted on being kept informed of even comparatively trivial matters, concerning legal disputes as well as
administrative issues, and either made unilateral decisions or
referred the case to the relevant authorities. At the height of his
political success his prestige was such that he rivalled the UrIII
kings in power and, like them, he was referred to as a god. His
popularity is also reflected in the names people gave their children,
such as 'Hammurabi is my help', or indeed 'Hammurabi is my god'.
On the whole though Old Babylonian kingship developed away
from the theocratic rule exercised by the kings of Ur. The kings
of Isin who regarded themselves to be the rightful heirs of Ur
encouraged the poets and scribes to compose royal hymns extolling
their closeness to the deities, including the consummation of
'marriage' to the city goddess.[16] The cult of reigning and defunct
kings was also gradually abandoned and Rim-Sin of Larsa broke
with many of the now obsolescent rituals and courtly customs. To
what extent this change reflects an egalitarian ethos of the originally tribal Amorite population remains questionable. In many ways
the ideological justification of kingship remained unchanged but
the attitudes towards the population, as the favoured metaphor
of the 'shepherd' shows, betrays a greater emphasis of a common
humanity and mutual responsibility which owes more to the way
a tribal sheikh functions than a semi-divine and exalted supreme
ruler at the apex of a hierarchical social structure.

The world of the Old Babylonian period has been memorably
characterised as a closed world in which 'people lived in a middle
class comfort of small towns and cities where private ownership was
dominant'.[17] Unless people happened to live in a zone of conflict
or ecological disaster, or at times of inter-city warfare and tribal
incursions, this was no doubt true for many parts of the country,
especially in the medium-sized and large urban centres. Archaeologists such as Sir Leonard Woolley at Ur have excavated a number
of comfortably appointed 'middle-class' homes, which belonged to
educated professionals or business people. They were spacious
dwellings, not unlike traditional houses in the Middle East from
the recent past, with high enclosures, internal courtyards, and even
bitumen-lined, terracotta-paved toilets and bathrooms.[18] The lively
activity of the scribal centres in cities such as Nippur, Babylon,
Sippar and Larsa is also an index of prosperity and peace. Altogether

the level of literary activity was exceptionally high during the Old Babylonian period. At no other times were so many letters exchanged between private individuals, and cuneiform schools were set up in most of the larger cities. On the other hand, the royal 'acts of justice', issued in greater frequency after Hammurabi's death, also hint at a less rosy picture of crushing debt burdens incurred through falling agricultural productivity and high interest rates on loan capital taken out to meet tax demands and other obligations. The royal act was meant to alleviate the worst problems by cancelling arrears payable to the state and erasing debts between private individuals. Debt slavery, whereby the debtor either offered himself or his dependants as work forces, was all too common.

By the end of the seventeenth century the ecological situation, especially in the south, seems to have worsened; elsewhere the lack of maintenance of important waterways and integrated defence systems became problematic.

There were also new waves of tribal immigrants. The Amorites had become either acculturated and settled or merged with other tribal pastoralist groups. A new people, also tribally organised and breeders of horses rather than sheep, had arrived from the east and settled in the east Tigris region. As new groups followed, they gradually moved further west into the middle Babylonian region and according to texts from Sippar and Babylon hired themselves out for seasonal labour as well as mercenaries. As long as they were relatively few in number and politically disunited, they were not seen to pose a problem but eventually, once they adopted more forceful ways of securing land and pasturage, they became a threat to established settlements. According to some year names, various successors of Hammurabi were obliged to campaign against these people whom they called Kassites but by the seventeenth century they appear firmly ensconced in the southern Jezirah up to the middle Euphrates region. However, it was not the Kassites who brought the First Dynasty of Babylon and the Old Babylonian period to a sudden end. It came from an unexpected part of the world, from Anatolia, where the Hittites, an Indo-European people, had made a swift and steady rise to form a powerful state. Having gained firm control over the Anatolian highlands, they set their sights further south, to the wealthy Syrian kingdom of Yamhad and the new Hurrian state in north-east Syria. In c. 1595 King

41

Mursili I attacked and destroyed Aleppo, the capital of Yamhad, as well as the fortified trading centre of Karkemish.[19] Spurred by this success he decided to target another famously rich city, Babylon. Since only the presence of the Kassites on the middle Euphrates could have blocked his way it is likely that he came to a mutual arrangement with their leaders. According to a Hittite chronicle, Mursili went to Babylon and occupied the city; he kept the prisoners and booty from Babylon at Hattusas (the Hittite capital in central Anatolia). Samsu-ditana, the Babylonian king, perhaps taken by surprise, seems to have offered little resistance. He lost his throne and presumably his life. This ended the First Dynasty of Babylon.

The demise of the Amorite Dynasty left the northern part of the country without effective government. Documentary evidence in southern cities had stopped before the fall of Babylon; the scribal quarter at Nippur was deserted already during the reign of Samsu-iluna (1749–1712). We have seen that some scribes and priests moved to northern cities while others found a place in the new kingdom in the marsh region. After the death of Samsu-ditana writing seems to have stopped also in the north. Historians are wont to call such periods 'dark ages', unilluminated by written records. The image of a dark age evokes a general break-down of civil order and widespread social disintegration. However, the absence of bureaucratic record-keeping and royal inscriptions does not necessarily imply a complete disruption of civil society. First of all there was the rapid re-establishment of writing as soon as a new stable government was securely in place, without any marked breaks in tradition. This would have been difficult to achieve after radical social change and upheavals. Secondly, while writing is an index of a particular form of urban culture which needed large institutional bodies and a certain level of prosperity to flourish, it is not essential for economic survival. The excavations at Nippur, for instance, have shown quite poignantly how the once grand houses of civil servants were subdivided to accommodate poorer relatives, how chicken coops and goat stalls filled every spare corner, and how the exercise 'books' were thrown out with the rubbish. Unemployed scribes and officials had to fall back on other modes of subsistence. The great cultural value of literacy, however, ensured that it was never totally abandoned despite its temporary lack of economic value. It has also been pointed out that it is notoriously difficult to determine the length of 'dark ages'. Not only are large parts of existing tablet collections still untouched and undated, but there remain many sites still unexcavated which could very well provide new sources – especially in the south of Mesopotamia, the region of the 'Sealand' is poorly known. Furthermore, the chronological sequence for the first part of the second millennium is provisional. According to new archaeologically based surveys, the Old Babylonian period may well have lasted a century longer, which would shorten the hiatus between the First Dynasty of Babylon and the Kassite Dynasty considerably. However long the actual break lasted, the Old Babylonian age more or less gradually came to an end by the middle of the second millennium.

THE MIDDLE BABYLONIAN PERIOD
(c. 1500–612)

The Kassites, who called themselves *galzu* (Akkadian *kaššu*),rrived in Mesopotamia from the east. It is not known where their ancestral homeland was and which route they took to reach Mesopotamia. Their familiarity with horses may give a clue that they came from the Eurasian steppe lands, but that could also have been acquired *en route*. They first appear as a people in the Babylonian records during the reign of Hammurabi's successor Samsu-iluna; his ninth year (1741) was named after a clash with Kassite forces. The Kassites settled in the east Tigris region and from there expanded westwards to take over the kingdom of Hana, in the middle Euphrates region, where they established their own polity whose centre was probably Terqa. When the Hittites launched their surprise march on Babylon, the Kassites could have blocked their way but they did not. Nor did they exploit the power vacuum left by the death of Samsu-ditana of Babylon. Conventional chronologies instead allow for a lapse of some 150 years before Babylon was taken by the Kassites. According to alternative suggestions though, which place the raid of Mursili at the beginning of the fifteenth century, the interval would have been much shorter.[20] Even so, it was a Sealand king, Gulkishar, who seized northern Babylonia first since his dynasty is counted as following the Amorite dynasty in the Babylonian King List A. However, the Kassites, led by a certain

Ulam-Buriash, decided to keep northern Babylonia under their control and they defeated the Sealand in c. 1475. Gulkishar had to retreat back to the far south. By the end of the fifteenth century this southern region also became integrated into the Kassite Babylonian state.

The Kassite dynasty was the longest lasting in all Babylonian history (c. 1600–1155) and their rule brought five hundred years of stability, prosperity and peace. The Kassite rulers chose a new centre as the hub of their state, at a strategic place now known as Aqar Quf, where the rivers Euphrates and Tigris came closest together (some 30 km west of modern Baghdad). The UrIII kings had already built a fortress there which was rebuilt by the Babylonian king Apil-Sin in the late nineteenth century. It was greatly expanded under the Kassite king Kurigalzu I at the end of the fifteenth and the beginning of the fourteenth century. He renamed it Dur-Kurigalzu (Fort of Kurigalzu). Babylon became the ceremonial and religious centre. The Kassite kings promoted the cult of the great Mesopotamian deities; they built and renewed the sanctuaries throughout the land and donated votive gifts. Little is known about the traditional Kassite religion except that the investiture of new kings took place in the shrine of two Kassite gods, Shumaliya and Shuqamuna.

Considering the length of the dynasty and the political equilibrium, the period is not well known either archaeologically or textually. Even when written sources are available, such as the collections of economic texts from Nippur, Ur and Babylon, they remain unpublished. No sizeable royal archives from the Kassite or later dynasties have yet been discovered. This means that the Middle Babylonian period is the least well-known epoch of Babylonian history. Most of the historically useful documents date from 1390 to 1190 and constitute some of the diplomatic correspondence with other royal houses of the period, notably Egypt, Hittite Anatolia and Assyria. A peculiarity of the Kassite dynasty were the conically shaped boundary stones (*kudurru*) which were erected to commemorate royal donations of land (Fig. 2.2). They were protected with

Figure 2.2 Boundary stone depicting the Kassite king Marduk-nadin ahhe. He wears a richly embroidered robe and a fez-like hat, c. 1090 BC. Above are the symbols of deities. (© British Museum)

symbols of deities and sometimes contain lengthy inscriptions which furnish precious details about contemporary society and historical events. For several centuries Babylonia suffered from civil unrest and foreign occupation and that is when written documentation almost ceased completely. Only the story of the struggle between Assyria and Babylonia is well known because of Assyrian royal annals and chronicles and because it interested later Babylonian historians.

Although the Kassite rulers always used Kassite names and were of foreign origin, they did not impose foreign customs on the people they governed. Nor was the elite entirely composed of their compatriots. It has often been remarked how complete the acculturation of the Kassite rulers to Mesopotamian traditions and customs was. At least this is the image they projected in their royal inscriptions which follow earlier precedents and use a time-honoured phraseology. They did not seem interested in expressing their own language in writing – only a few phrases, mainly those used in personal names, were translated by Babylonian lexicographers. Instead, they promoted and encouraged the existing scribal traditions and learning. It was after all during this time that Babylonian became the diplomatic language of the whole Near East. There were no breaks in the religious and cultic institutions since the kings again followed the example of their predecessors and fulfilled their obligations towards the restoration and renewal of temple buildings. It is in fact impossible from the available texts to detect any specific 'Kassite' or 'foreign' traits. This may mean that the Kassites were not interested in shaping the intellectual or cultural expression of the land they ruled and did not actively seek to influence it; that they left such matters to the indigenous literary elite. There is also the possibility that they chose to leave their mark by other means, by maintaining a tight grip on actual power in order to reshape the country in more profound ways without having to invent new forms of legitimisation.

The most important change from the Old Babylonian period was the transition from political fragmentation to a national monarchy who ruled over a territory with clear borders. Once the Sealand had been captured and integrated in the late fifteenth century, the Babylonian state under the Kassites reached from the southern marshes to the middle Euphrates region, roughly covering the extent of Hammurabi's empire. This unification was no short-lived attempt at centralisation, such as the Akkadian kingdom or the UrIII state, but it became the norm for centuries. The Kassite monarchy thus instigated this process which was to end the previous system of particularism and small city-states once and for all. Thereafter Babylonia could be subject to other states, notably Assyria, but it remained a distinct political entity.

By the middle of the second millennium, a new era was beginning which drew the world of the whole ancient Near East closer together. This was not least due to technological changes in warfare and particularly to the use of horse-drawn chariots and vehicles which allowed troops to move at greater speed and with more agility. New state formations arose in Anatolia, north-east Syria, Elam and Egypt and they all looked beyond their borders to the fertile and wealthy regions of the Near East which was to become a source of tribute revenue for competing powers.

The lands north of the border, in western Syria right down to the east Tigris region, were occupied by the Hurrians, another people from the east, who had settled in large numbers and mixed with the local population and west Semitic tribal immigrants. Like in Babylonia, the political power there was in the hands of a 'foreign' elite, the Mitanni. Like the Kassites, they had come from the east, and seem to have made political capital from their familiarity with horses and chariots. The ruling elite (they called themselves *Mariannu*) spoke an Indo-European language although the main language was Hurrian. Their kingdom, known as Mitanni, became subject to tribute payments to the Hittites who ruled from Anatolia. It was finally conquered by the Assyrians who had established themselves as a new political power under king Ashur-uballit I (c. 1365–1245). Assyria subsequently became a threat to Babylonia.

In the east, the Elamite dynasty of Eparti was much reduced in power and the circumstances of the dynasty's end remain uncertain since no written sources are preserved beyond 1500. The political fortunes of Elam revived only in the last quarter of the second millennium. It was therefore not a major player during the best-documented phase of the Kassite period. Much more important, though no immediate neighbour of Babylonia, was Egypt. Pharaohs of the 18th Dynasty, particularly Tuthmosis I (1493–1483), extended Egyptian influence well into western Asia, along the coast of Syria–Palestine. This expansion brought Egypt into a wider political and economic network, thus ending centuries of isolation. By the fourteenth century pharaohs and the kings of the larger states (Babylonia, Hatti, Mitanni and Assyria) entered into cumbersome but effective diplomatic relations which helped to maintain overall stability in the Near East for some 150 years.

As far as one can tell from the still fragmentary written sources, mainly from the fourteenth and thirteenth centuries, Babylonia under Kassite rule was a well-organised, highly centralised state. The government invested in infrastructure and especially irrigation works in order to boost agricultural production. The country was divided into provinces administered by senior officials appointed by the king. These officials were responsible for the collection of taxes and public works. The administrative system generally favoured centralisation – there were fewer and larger urban centres surrounded by their productive areas under cultivation, fields, orchards and pastures. At the same time there were many villages so that some 57 per cent of the settled area was rural rather than urban.[21] Some cities, notably Sippar and Babylon, had special privileges and a separate tax status.

Taxes were raised from almost everything: on all produce of fields and gardens – grain, fodder, straw, dates and so on; from animal husbandry, hunting and fishing; from trade and craft income and so on. The sums that were collected from these revenues were colossal. Furthermore the population had to provide services and transport for military and civilian purposes, such as the construction and maintenance of irrigation and other hydraulic works, roads, city walls, fortifications and so on. This general practice of corvée labour also allowed for the major cities and their major buildings to be kept in good repair.

Babylonia was a wealthy country at that time, not least because of its pivotal place within the long-distance trade which passed through its territory, from north to south and east to west. The opening-up of Egypt as an active business partner was an enormous gain to Babylonia. Egypt depended on the Near East for all manner of goods, while timber and copper were obtained from Syria–Palestine and Cyprus respectively. Both regions were subject to tribute payments but also traded with Egypt. Babylonia supplied most of the semi-precious stones and the much coveted lapis lazuli from the Iranian east, but also exported horses, richly worked and finished textiles, jewellery and other luxury items. The most prized Egyptian commodity was gold, which was found nowhere else at the time. In Babylonia it replaced the customary silver as the standard of equivalence for a century and a half!

This prosperity was further safeguarded by the Kassite rulers' cautious foreign policy. With few exceptions, such as the raid of Elam by Kurigalzu II, they did not engage in aggressive warfare and preferred to defend their borders. It has also been pointed out that the dispersal of the population in rural settlements, combined with the efficient organisation of the military, made Babylonia better able to absorb any foreign attack and tribal immigration.[22] The self-sufficiency of Babylonia stands in contrast with the expansionism of the northern states. Both the Hittite and the Assyrian kingdoms relied on forceful territorial annexations of productive regions beyond their homeland to supply foodstuff and payments in silver. This dependence made these states vulnerable to resistance and rebellion, quite apart from the fact that they faced competition from other states in similar circumstances. The struggles between Mitanni, Hatti and Assyria can be explained because of this dynamic.

Babylonia was not involved in the competition over foreign territory. On the other hand, it was an active partner in the diplomatic games of one-upmanship which pitted one 'super-power' of the day against another as documented in royal correspondence of the Amarna period (see below).

The political stability and economic prosperity of Kassite Babylonia – at least in the fourteenth and thirteenth centuries – favoured the literary professions. Although the Old Babylonian Tablet Houses did not survive into this period, the training of scribes was either carried out in the old temple academies, particularly at Nippur and Babylon, or by private individuals. The scholars of the previous period had put much effort into preserving the Sumerian literary heritage by translating lexical lists and important compositions. The Middle Babylonian scribes were concerned mainly with the consolidation of Akkadian literature, sometimes referred to as the canonisation or standardisation phase. Sumerian became a technical language the use of which was restricted to the most esoteric subjects and some cultic texts. New lexical lists, such as those which enumerate synonyms, were compiled at this time. The few remaining examples of Kassite vocabulary, especially those relating to horse breeding, derive from such lists. The Gilgamesh Epic was worked into a coherent narrative, and of great importance were also literary prayers. In contrast to the Old Babylonian period, writing appears altogether more professional and less available to ordinary citizens. There are far fewer private letters for instance, although this may of course be a result of our fragmentary sources. One has the impression that in Babylonia writing was the privilege of an educated elite who passed the craft on among their own class. This raised status was surely reflected in the remuneration of their services which moved them out of reach for all but the wealthy and the institutions. The same process can be seen with other professions. Disciplines such as incantation 'science', astronomy, medicine, exorcism and divination also became more professionalised and practitioners had to undergo a lengthy training to qualify since familiarity with written standard works became mandatory. This produced a large gap between the trained, lettered and official practitioners and those who relied on oral and traditional folk methods. One of the results of the higher status of Babylonian professionals was the great respect they commanded well beyond the confines of Mesopotamia. Babylonian intellectuals became a highly valued export since Babylonian learning was admired and coveted in all other regions of the Near East which aspired to achieve sophistication. Only Egypt rivalled Babylonia for its expert physicians and diviners. But since Egyptian culture was inherently more self-contained and imbued with a sense of superiority, Egyptian intellectuals were loath to initiate their uncouth neighbours into their arcane world of knowledge. The Babylonians had no such scruples and, furthermore, there was a long Mesopotamian tradition of extending the range of literacy further afield. This explains why it was Babylonian and not Egyptian that became the *lingua franca* for the whole of the Near East from the fifteenth to the end of the thirteenth century. The standard cuneiform reference works, such as sign lists, syllabaries and lexical lists, were found in many archaeological sites of the region: from the Hattusas, the Hittite capital in central Anatolia, to cities in Syria and the Levant, as well as Egypt. Here the most important find spot was the new capital Akhetaten (modern el Amarna), built by Amenhotep IV who changed his name to Akhenaten. Babylonian scribes were much in demand at foreign courts though they also trained local people using the lexical lists which were often given an extra column with translations into the local idiom. Syrian, Hittite and Egyptian apprentice scribes, just like their Babylonian counterparts, had to acquire some familiarity with the great works of Mesopotamian literature; some excerpts of the Gilgamesh Epic for instance have been found in far-flung places.

The widespread contacts with foreign places and peoples helped to extend the cultural horizon of professionals and the ruling elite. Through the medium of the Babylonian language the rulers of powerful kingdoms communicated directly with each other. Those letters which were directed to and received by the pharaoh of Egypt were discovered among the ruins of the pharaonic records office at Amarna, some 380 tablets altogether, dating from a period of no longer than some thirty years (c. 1390–1363).[23] The majority concern Egyptian vassals in the Levant; 43 were written by the rulers of Hatti, Mitanni, Assyria and Babylonia and Alashiya (Cyprus). The letters were written in the flowery language of diplomacy but with graduations in the degree of intimacy each ruler thought to have established with the pharaoh. This was mainly engineered through gift exchange, with the most prized offers being chariots and well-trained horses, princesses, embroidered robes and textiles, and other high-luxury commodities. Egypt was expected to reciprocate primarily with gold, which as one correspondent insisted 'was as common as sand' in Egypt. The Kassite king Burnaburiash wrote several letters complaining about the slow and meagre response from the pharaoh and in his eagerness to gain points over his Near Eastern rivals he even suggests that a less-than-royal female be sent as a substitute for a real pharaoh's daughter. The letters show how keenly the Kassite kings engaged in the competition for status. Although the diplomatic letters exchanged by the members of the 'Great Powers Club' make use of the metaphor of a small village community, where the various great kings relate to each other as 'brothers',[24] there was also a recognition of differences in custom, outlook and ideological systems. As such they played an important role in furthering mutual understanding in the Near East and to mitigate somewhat against the relative isolation of Babylonia.

Technological innovations were disseminated quite quickly, such as the use of horses in warfare and the construction of manoeuvrable fast chariots, or glass making which was probably invented in coastal Syria. Furthermore the awareness of economic and political interdependence opened the doors to collaboration and compromise instead of violent confrontation, although this was by no means always the case and by the end of the thirteenth century, the 150 years of peace came to end.

In Anatolia the Hittite kingdom collapsed about 1200, the capital having been attacked and destroyed by an as yet unnamed enemy. At the same time there was similar devastation further east, in Mycenaean Greece and Cyprus. In the Levant a number of wealthy but vulnerable kingdoms such as Ugarit in coastal Syria were swept away. These devastations caused massive population displacements which spread disruption. By the middle of the twelfth century Egypt faced a seaborne invasion by an enemy described only as the 'sea people' – and although Rameses III was able to quell their attacks he could not hold on to the Egyptian possessions in the Levant. In older historical accounts of the period these mysterious 'sea people' were summarily blamed for both the collapse of the Hittite state and the levels of devastation throughout the eastern Mediterranean. It has since become clear that there was no single ethnic or political group that could conveniently be held responsible. Instead, a variety of factors contributed to the deterioration of stability, although they are still poorly understood. Anatolia seems to have experienced ecological problems, and there were famines in preceding periods and repeated attacks by populations either subject to Hatti or newcomers which weakened internal control. In Syria, the centuries of Egyptian, Mitanni and Hittite exploitation had also left their mark and the violent clashes between Egypt and Hatti, culminating in the battle of Qadesh, caused widespread disruption. The ruling elites of Syrian and Palestinian cities were bound to fulfil their tribute obligations to their overlords, Egyptian or Hittite, and protected by their garrisons enriched themselves in the process to the detriment of the local populations. The Amarna letters speak of social unrest caused by dispossessed small farmers and pastoralists. It appears that Egypt was reluctant to interfere unless its own interests were threatened. This made the wealthy urban cities who were often dependent on foreign garrison protection vulnerable to attacks. Once the Hittite control had gone, one Syrian city after another became a target for destruction and large-scale looting, destabilising the whole region. In the subsequent centuries, the local population – now associated with the term 'Aramean' – reverted back to the pattern of small independent city-states and territories under the control of sheikhs.

The political situation in the Near East changed profoundly.[25] With the disappearance of the Hittites and the Egyptians from the scene, the centre of gravity shifted from west to east, where Assyria and Elam began to dominate the fate of Babylonia in a decisive manner.

Assyria had steadily risen to greater influence ever since the reign of Ashur-uballit I (1365–1330), a fact which caused considerable discomfort to the Babylonians although the Assyrian monarch sealed the mutual tolerance by marrying his daughter to the Babylonian crown prince. This family connection legitimised Assyrian intervention during a Babylonian *coup d'état* but generally the two neighbouring countries coexisted quite peacefully. This changed when the Assyrian monarch Tukulti-Ninurta I (1244–1197) came to power. He was one of the first warrior kings whose main concern was to enlarge Assyrian territories and influence. This could be achieved only by almost continuous military campaigns and by concentrating resources on the army and fortifications. One of the main reasons for this aggressive policy was to secure privileged access to trade goods, such as copper, tin, horses, and semi-precious stones such as lapis lazuli for which Assyria had to compete with other Near Eastern states, especially Babylon. Tukulti-Ninurta marched into Hittite territory (where copper was mined) and fought a victorious battle where he claimed to have captured 28,000 prisoners. He set up a number of control points on trade routes and finally decided to settle matters with Babylonia which had meanwhile taken possession of border territory on its northern frontier. This gave Tukulti-Ninurta an opportunity to attack his southern neighbours and defeat them in battle. The Babylonian king Kashtiliash IV was taken to Ashur in chains. This defeat initiated direct Assyrian control over Babylonia which was to last thirty-two years. The liberation of the country had to wait until Assyria was weakened by internal power struggles following Tukulti-Ninurta's death. A Babylonian king, Adad-shuma-usur (1216–1187), who had established a base in the Sealand, was able to drive out the Assyrian puppet ruler in Babylon and imprison the Assyrian king. However, a new dangerous situation arose from the east, from a revitalised Elam which also tried to assert control over Babylonia. This sparked a conflict with Assyria that was to remain a constant feature of Elamite politics for the next 500 years. The Elamite king Kiden-Hutran (1235–c. 1210) invaded Babylonia, destroyed Der, conquered Nippur and replaced the Assyrian regent with one appointed by Elam. The raids were continued under subsequent Elamite kings in order to weaken Assyrian influence in Babylonia. The climax was a massive invasion by Elamite troops under the leadership of Shutruk-Nahhunte I (c. 1158). According to the Babylonian Chronicle, the city of Babylon was devastated and most of the great cities plundered. The Elamites also took with them ancient monuments, such as the stele with Hammurabi's Law Code, and much to the inhabitants' distress, the statues of Babylonian gods, including those of Marduk and his consort Sarpanitum. The Elamites also asserted their control over the whole of eastern Mesopotamia. The Babylonians, led by their king Enlil-nadin-ahhe, rebelled against the son and successor of Shutruk-Nahhunte, but the Babylonian king Enlil-nadin-ahhe, the last of the long line of Kassite rulers, was killed (c. 1155).

Under the impact of the Elamite invasion the centre of political activism and resistance in Babylonia now moved much further south, to the city of Isin – home of the 'Second Dynasty of Isin' of the king list. One of their kings, Nebuchadnezzar I (1125–1104),[26] mounted a counter-attack on Elam and succeeded in defeating the Elamite king. His victory is described at length not in an official royal inscription but in a land grant document issued by one of Nebuchadnezzar's officials, who commanded the decisive charge. One of the consequences of this victory was the return of the cult statues of Marduk and Sarpanitum to Babylon, an event that did much to restore the morale of the Babylonian population. Since the reign of the Kassites, Babylon had been the ceremonial and religious centre of the country where the New Year Festival was celebrated. This complex ritual, which involved the gathering of all important Babylonian deities at Babylon, the recitation of the Creation Epic (*enuma elish*) and the confirmation of kingship by the god Marduk, was given new impetus, if it was not altogether invented at this time, as some scholars claim, by Nebuchadnezzar I. Certainly the ritual of the king grasping the hands of Marduk became a significant component after the return of the statues from their Elamite exile. There was also a spurt of literary and scholarly creativity – hymns and songs, omens and astronomical observations were written down at this time, many of which were still consulted hundreds of years later. Nebuchadnezzar's royal inscriptions stress his reverence for the traditional Mesopotamian notion of responsible kingship, with a strong patronage of scribal arts and the cult of Babylonian deities. He did much to raise confidence and self-esteem in the country so that subsequent generations of scribes lauded him as an exemplary king, much like Sargon and Hammurabi before him, and also, a significant point, as a successful liberator from foreign oppression.

Having regained political independence from its neighbouring states, Babylonia was torn apart by internal political instability, the result of competition between tribal leaders vying for power. The next two hundred years were a difficult period for Babylonia, marked by the influx of tribal groups from the east and internal fragmentation. Short-lived 'dynasties' tried to secure some form of Babylonian independence and legitimacy. The major problem of the eleventh and tenth centuries was the incursions of semi-nomadic peoples, such as the Arameans and Suteans.[27] The underlying causes for the massive displacement of peoples are not clearly understood; whether they were primarily due to climatic problems causing prolonged drought in western Syria or were triggered by the unrest and violent events in the Mediterranean region around 1200.[28] There are hardly any written sources from Babylonia for this time, especially the tenth century, but later Babylonian chronicles blamed Arameans and Suteans for having ransacked the country and even targeted the temples of major cities, such as Uruk, Nippur and Sippar.

After the collapse of the Isin Dynasty the centre of control shifted to the south where the 'Second Sealand Dynasty' (1026–1006) was initiated by a man with a Kassite name, Simbar-Sipak, who managed to rule for eighteen years until he was assassinated. The next dynasty, known as the House of Bazi (1005–986), had its base further east in the Tigris region. Then an Elamite occupied the Babylonian throne for six years, and after this came a succession of some twenty kings bracketed in poorly documented dynasties. However, despite the problems caused by tribal invasions and the disruption of the economy owing to raids on crops and the lack of safety on trade routes, there were intermittent periods of relative stability. Nabu-mukin-apli, the first ruler of the so-called Dynasty E, even enjoyed a reign for thirty-five years (979–944). During the ninth century the tribal peoples had become settled in small groups on more or less marginal land, away from the major cities. Once again, the Babylonian urban society had survived a major incursion of semi-nomadic peoples and the slow process of assimilation had begun. Another tribal group, the so-called Chaldeans, had also established themselves in the marshland region of the south, the old Sealand. Unlike the often impoverished Arameans, the Chaldeans became extremely wealthy, thanks to their control over the southern trade routes through the Arabian peninsula and the Persian Gulf.

Relations between Babylonian and Assyrian kings during most of the ninth century were marked by quite intensive contacts, sometimes hostile but often collaborative. There were some marriage alliances and some intervention in the face of palace intrigues and attempted coups. The Assyrian kings were generally occupied with the expansion of their empire to the north and north-east, in Anatolia, Syria and the Zagros region, and the consolidation of their conquests.

The 33-year-long reign of Nabu-apla-iddina, who acceded the throne in c. 870, marked a high point of Babylonian importance. The Arameans were no longer a threat, he had defeated the Suteans and deflected their activities to the detriment of his Assyrian neighbours and the country enjoyed a period of prosperity and peace, helped by a treaty with Shalmaneser III. Written sources become more plentiful for this period and the contemporary inscriptions praise the king for the restoration of temples and the reactivating of disrupted cult services throughout the land. However, this state of affairs was not to last for long. Although the Babylonian king Marduk-zakir-shumi had helped Shamshi-Adad V to the Assyrian throne following a palace revolt which pitted one brother against the other, the terms of his involvement were considered humiliating to the Assyrian party. Shamshi-Adad turned against Babylonia in three successive campaigns which ended in the deportation of the Babylonian king to Nineveh. A period of anarchy followed in Babylonia, while Assyria's power rose throughout the Near East.

The unstable situation in Babylonia proved problematic for the Assyrians who were also vulnerable to the spread of tribal unrest. The energetic Assyrian king Adad-nirari III (810–783) attempted to solve this danger and initiated a policy towards Babylonia which was to remain typical for the ensuing relations between the two countries; while the more powerful Assyrians would assume more or less direct control over all political affairs in Babylonia, dictating the borders, appointing rulers or even assuming kingship, they were also at pains to proclaim their respect for the holy cities of the country and especially for the god Nabu whose cult enjoyed great popularity in the Assyrian cities. The Babylonians – according to the Babylonian Chronicles – saw the Assyrians as oppressors and as soon as an opportunity arose they were quick to seize it in order to shake off their yoke. Thus Eriba-Marduk, a Chaldean tribal leader, assumed the Babylonian throne in c. 770 when another revolution shook the Assyrian palace at Calah after the death of Adad-nirari III. On the other hand, the Assyrian interventions were directed against tribal groups who were destabilising the country-side and the cities, and although the Assyrians took away the spoils, especially when they defeated wealthy tribes like those in the south, Babylonia profited from their pacification. Thus any temporary weakening of Assyrian control gave rise to intense internal competition for the Babylonian throne. Such rivalries contributed finally to the imposition of direct Assyrian rule which was to persist for some hundred years (from 729 to 627). It was also related to the spectacular growth of Assyrian power which was initiated by Tiglath-Pileser III (744–727). Having expanded his empire to the north-east (victory over the Urartians), consolidated his hold on Syria, and subdued the troublesome Manneans in the east, he needed to settle the Babylonian problem. After the relatively peaceful reign of Nabu-nasir (747–734) the country was again troubled by regicide and Chaldean coups. Tiglath-Pileser defeated their incumbant on the Babylonian throne (Nabu-mukin-zeri) and in order to put an end to further unrest, proclaimed himself king of Babylonia in 729, made manifest by his participation in the New Year Festival in Babylon. This allowed for the 'double monarchy' to be regarded as officially legitimate in Babylonia. However, the assumption of

Assyrian rule did not dampen the aspirations of the Chaldean leaders. On the contrary they could now assume the roles of fighters for the Babylonian 'national' cause and they were skilful in allying themselves to other groups who equally resented the might of Assyria, such as Elam which had risen in importance, and the various western Semitic tribes, including the Arabs upon whom the Assyrians had imposed hefty tribute payments. Thus it was already during the reign of Tiglath-Pileser's successor, Sargon II (721–705), that the leader of the Chaldean Bit-Yakin tribe, Marduk-apla-iddina, with military support from Elam, defeated an Assyrian army and installed himself as king of Babylon for some ten years (721–710). This was only possible while Sargon was occupied elsewhere, quelling revolts in the Syrian vassal states and subduing the Urartians in south-east Anatolia. As soon as all this was accomplished he turned his attention to Babylonia and ousted Marduk-apla-iddina who went into exile in Elam. Sargon then assumed the royal title of king of Babylonia and kept a firm grip on the country. His sudden death on a military campaign sparked further rebellions. Babylonia seized the opportunity to make a bid for independence under a new king who was swiftly replaced by Marduk-apla-iddina who had come back from Elam. The Babylonian problem and his hatred for Marduk-apla-iddina was to become the main preoccupation of Sargon's son Sennacherib (704–681) and ended in disaster for Babylonia. Sennacherib chased the Chaldean from Babylon and then, for reasons which are largely unclear, he decided not to continue with the double monarchy and appointed an Assyrian puppet ruler, a Babylonian noble called Bel-ibni who had been brought up in Assyria, to the Babylonian throne instead. The latter seems to have been won over by the anti-Assyrian faction and duly rebelled in 700. Sennacherib was forced to intervene again and to put down further revolts in the south. This time he appointed his own son and crown-prince, Ashur-nadin-shumi, as king of Babylonia. He then directed his attention to the southern marshes in order to get hold of Marduk-apla-iddina who was at the time in his home base around Bit-Yakin. This was in turn exploited by the Elamite king who made a surprise attack on Sippar in northern Babylonia and captured and deported Ashur-nadin-shumi to Elam where the Assyrian prince probably died. The Elamites appointed their own king over Babylonia, and for good measure inflicted a defeat on the Assyrian forces. Although Sennacherib managed to reverse the situation and capture the Elamite pretender to the Babylonian throne, he needed to mount a massive campaign against Elam and its allies which resulted in an inconclusive battle. Meanwhile another Chaldean leader had assumed Babylonian kingship, causing Sennacherib to turn his attention to the city of Babylon which was taken after a bloody 15-month siege in 689. According to his own inscriptions, the Assyrian king vented his fury on the defeated city, carried the Babylonian ruler and his family to captivity, plundered the temple treasuries, deported or smashed the statues of the gods and flooded the city by means of a specially dug canal. The scale of the destruction wrought on Babylon may have been exaggerated in these inscriptions but the removal of the Marduk statue and the discontinuity of temple services were seen as particularly disruptive by later Babylonian writers. Sennacherib was assassinated in a palace intrigue and one of his sons, Esarhaddon (680–669) became king. His attitude to Babylonia was marked by a sense of guilt over his father's behaviour and his policy was to try and make amends. He ordered the deported statues of Babylonian gods to be repaired and repatriated, though the return of the god Marduk was not effected until his son's reign; he allowed Babylonian deportees to return home and invested in the restoration of temples in the ancient cities. The kingship over Babylonia was entrusted to Assyrian appointees. Such measures were no doubt welcomed by senior temple officials and the senior dignitaries but the general mood in the country was strongly anti-Assyrian, albeit without a united front. The Chaldeans were the most virulent opposition, although factionalism and internal rivalries rendered their activities often counter-productive. Elam at that time had also turned its back on Babylonia, and there was even a ferocious Elamite attack on Sippar culminating in a massacre of the inhabitants. In order to solve both the question of the problematic Assyrian succession to the throne and the matter of legitimate sovereignty in Babylonia, Esarhaddon thought of a novel solution which was to prove even more calamitous for the southern country. He announced that his elder son Shamash-shumu-ukin was to be king of Babylonia while the younger son Ashurbanipal should rule Assyria. When Esarhaddon died in 669 his mother Naqi'a-Zakutu asserted her considerable influence to ensure that the succession proceded smoothly. It soon became clear that Ashurbanipal (668–c. 631) wielded far greater power than his brother and that he continued to treat Babylonia as an Assyrian dependency. Although he carried on his father's programme of restoration it did little to stem the growing resistance to Assyrian power. Shamash-shumu-ukin himself became caught up in the cause and ended up leading a massive uprising against his brother, having secured the assistance of Aramean, Arab and Elamite contingents, which lasted for two years (650–648). The Assyrians were forced into numerous military engagements across a wide territory. This caused considerable disruption to the agricultural production and the Babylonian population suffered severe famine. Finally Babylon fell in 648 after a two-year siege and Shamash-shumu-ukin died in his burning palace. Ashurbanipal re-asserted Assyrian control over the country and appointed an individual named Kandalanu (647–627) as king of Babylonia.[29] The next twenty years were comparatively peaceful and allowed the Babylonian economy to make a rapid recovery: agricultural production was stepped up and even long-distance trade revived. It was a period of respite although rival factions continued to vie for political influence. When Kandalanu died in 627 the succession of Nabopolassar was violently contested for several years although he eventually managed not only to secure his position on the throne but to mount a persistent and finally victorious attack on Assyria. This was made possible through the support of a new player on the Near Eastern scene, the Medes, who had become a powerful force in eastern Iran. Assyria itself had begun to weaken after a century of imperial policy which had displaced millions of people from one region to another. It relied on relentless punitive expeditions to put down rebellions which arose at any sign of loosening control. Finally the very success of Assyria might have contributed to its downfall, such as Ashurbanipal's decisive victory over Elam in 646, which cleared the way to Median penetration of the region, or the conquest of Egypt which demanded a heavy investment in troops and resources. Nabopolassar's struggle against Assyria was at first a continuation of old liberation wars against the northern oppressor but he targeted Assyrian provinces, first along the Euphrates right up to the Balikh river region, and then in the east Tigris area up to the Zab. He had to fight tenaciously, repelling Assyrian resistance along the way.

By 615 he had even penetrated into Assyrian heartland and, with Median support, threatened the city of Ashur but had to withdraw. However, it signalled a possibility of a direct strike against the centre of Assyrian power which was taken up by the Medes the very next year. This time they started an unsuccessful attack on the capital Nineveh and then captured and sacked the old ceremonial centre, the city of Ashur. The Babylonians arrived late but Nabopolassar concluded a treaty with the Median king Cyaxares for mutual support. Three years later, in 612, the two armies met again to launch a concerted attack on Nineveh. The city was taken after a two-month siege. The remnant of the Assyrian government moved its headquarters much further north, to Harran. Nineveh was devastated and huge booty was carried off by the Median and Babylonian victors. This 'terrible defeat' as the Babylonian Chronicle calls it marked the end of Assyrian imperial power and an end to the political importance of the great cities of Assyria. It did not mark the end of imperialism in the Near East since the Babylonians were quick to occupy the former Assyrian provinces and assert their control over the subject populations in southern Anatolia, Syria and the Mediterranean coast, but excluding Egypt itself. This could be achieved only by forceful military engagements on several fronts and the main personage responsible for the relatively rapid success of these operations (from 609 to 605) was Nabopolassar's son Nebuchadnezzar. By the time he followed his father on the throne, Babylonia was well on the way to replacing Assyria as the main imperial power in the Near East. This initiated the final phase of Babylonian history, the Neo-Babylonian period, which was to see some hundred years of imperial glory and the incorporation of Babylonia within the next empires, first that of the Achaemenid Persians and then the Hellenistic kingdoms of Alexander's successors.

THE NEO- AND LATE BABYLONIAN PERIODS (c. 604 BC–141 AD)[30]

The long struggle of the Babylonians against the Assyrian hegemony had culminated in the destruction of Nineveh in 612. Nabopolassar, the Babylonian king who had won the war with the substantial help of his Median allies, initiated a new dynasty whose most illustrious ruler was his son Nebuchadnezzar II (604–562).[31] In the early years of his career when he accompanied Nabopolassar on campaigns as crown prince and in the aftermath of his succession to the Babylonian throne, he proved himself as an able military leader and his frequent campaigns assured that the various former Assyrian provinces were won for the Babylonians. His greatest rivals for the possessions in Syria and the Levant were the Egyptians. The Saitic Dynasty, which had followed the Nubian rulers who had been defeated by Assyria, contested the Babylonian bid for territories which had in former times been subject to Egypt. It is well known from the Biblical accounts how local rulers in trying to play out one power against another could become fatally entangled. Although some Levantine cities, notably Tyre, fought long and hard to ward off the Babylonians, their resistance proved ultimately fruitless and Babylonia came into the possession of the whole region and its considerable wealth. Furthermore, the imposed peace throughout the region stimulated long-distance commerce which could pass unhindered from the Mediterranean to the Iranian plateau, from the Persian Gulf to the Anatolian highlands. The revenue from taxes and tributes, trade and the newly flourishing agriculture in Babylonia was so substantial that the king found it expedient to invest these riches in massive building projects of which the capital Babylon was to benefit in the most spectacular manner. While Nebuchadnezzar proved himself to be a worthy successor of the Assyrian soldier kings, owing to his prowess on the battlefield and his indefatigable campaigning – unlike his Babylonian predecessors he was not quite as reticent to flaunt his triumph in his royal inscriptions – he demonstrated his allegiance to Babylonian custom in the lavish care he spent on the temples and shrines of the country and the beautification of Babylon. The Assyrian kings had always deployed vast sums in building themselves new palaces and administrative capitals, but Babylonia, despite occasional reparations, had suffered neglect during the centuries of occupation. Now was the time to make good the scars inflicted by Assyrian aggression and Babylon was to eclipse the former glory of Nineveh, now in ruins. In fact, the destruction of Babylon by Sennacherib came to be interpreted as the sacrilege which had led to the downfall of Assyria. The new dynasty was seen not only as the avenger of Babylon's humiliation but as the rightful heirs of Assyrian power. Nebuchadnezzar's works in the city were on a truly grandious scale: the new city walls, of double construction wide enough for two teams of chariots, encircled some three square miles. The Euphrates, which flowed right through the city, had its banks strengthened with mighty walls of baked brick and new palaces were erected near the city gates at the southern and northern ends. The most important monuments were the sacred precinct of Marduk and the Processional Way which linked the temple to the Ishtar Gate. It was to become the splendid setting for the celebration of the old New Year Festival which had assumed a cosmic importance with Babylonia's imperial status. The vast enclosure, surrounded by buttressed walls, contained the main temple of Marduk, as well as chapels for other Mesopotamian deities. The ziggurat Etemenanki, 'the foundation of heaven and earth', stood in the centre of the temenos, a vast structure composed of seven stages. On the top-most platform were the bed-chambers of the gods, and priests and attendants could reach the platform by a series of ramps and stairs. At least this is the impression we have based on the description of Herodotus, who had probably not been to Babylon himself, and various cuneiform reports, since there is no archaeological confirmation for the building's superstructure. The ziggurat was no doubt a landmark which could be seen from afar and it signalled the importance of Babylonian religious continuity and the cosmic importance of the sacred city. Such aspects were also performed ritually, especially during the New Year Festival, when all the major gods of the country were assembled in Babylon. On this occasion Marduk and the other deities, normally accommodated in Esagila, journeyed by boat to the so-called Festival House beyond the city gates, to return after the week-long rituals through the Ishtar Gate and along the Processional Road. This was the reason for the lavish architectural decorations executed in glazed tiles, with sacred emblems of Marduk's dragon, Ishtar's lions, and the bulls of the weather god Adad. Some portions of the wall surfaces have been reconstructed in the Pergamon Museum in Berlin, using the many thousands of fragments of the original tiles which the German excavator Robert Koldewey had discovered.[32]

During his 43-year reign Nebuchadnezzar engaged in ceaseless building activities – the construction of the ziggurat alone, initiated by his father Nabopolassar, went on for more than four decades – palaces and river embankments, fortified gates and the monumental city walls, as well as numerous temples apart from the Marduk sanctuary. Thousands of the square-shaped bricks, stamped with his name and titles, were found intact after some two and a half thousand years. All this effort was to demonstrate the unrivalled position of Babylon as the capital of a world power which had triumphed over its rivals Assyria and Egypt because of the divine will of Marduk. The official inscriptions, which mainly commemorated building projects, reiterated the traditional Mesopotamian view of kingship that while the king's position on earth reflected that of Marduk in heaven he was appointed to this office through the command of the gods.

Nebuchadnezzar's political struggles to build up and consolidate the Babylonian supremacy are hardly mentioned in contemporary sources; only some chronicles and legal texts point to internal revolts that were successfully repressed. After the king's death in 562, the dynastic succession could not be upheld for long because of intense palace rivalries. Some of his descendants did accede to the throne but only lasted for a few years: his son Amel-Marduk reigned two years before being assassinated by his brother-in-law Neriglissar (559–556), who in turn died after three years' rule, leaving a minor on the throne, who was quickly deposed by a palace intrigue which put Nabu-na'id (Nabonidus) (555–539) on the throne. He was not connected to the royal family and it has been suggested that his son Bel-shar-usur, better known by his Biblical sobriquet as Belshazzar, may have been involved in the coup. Nabonidus was probably of Aramean origin. His mother, an astonishingly long-lived lady called Addu-Guppi – she was said to have lived to the age of 102 and seemed to have come from Harran, the last Assyrian capital – later assumed a position at the Babylonian court during Nebuchadnezzar's and his successors' reigns. Nabonidus may also have been a courtier, and perhaps also a military commander, and was already in his sixties when he became king.[33] He was eager to legitimate his rule by practising the time-honoured conventions of royal patronage, especially rebuilding sanctuaries and investing in public restoration programmes. His particular reverence for the moon god is well known, and the rebuilding of his temple at Harran, which had been destroyed by the Medes, was the king's most cherished project. Some of Nabonidus' policies which used to be interpreted as grounded in a rather fanatical religious devotion to the moon god are now considered to have been driven by much more pragmatic military and economic considerations.

He strengthened the Babylonian defence at the northern margins of his empire to counter any expansionist moves of the Medes who had already conquered large parts of Anatolia. The other new threat was posed by Persian rulers who claimed descent from a certain Achaemenes and who had begun to contest the Median supremacy of eastern Iran. This event also curtailed any significant expansion by Medes to the detriment of Babylonian territories. Between 553 and 543 Nabonidus stayed away from Babylon, at the oasis town of Teima. This was an unusually prolonged absence of a Babylonian king from his capital and the celebration of the New Year Festival had to be suspended for all this time. Nabonidus' move to Arabia, perhaps initially motivated by ideas for imperial expansion, may also have been driven by the desire to incorporate this extremely wealthy region. While the Assyrians, especially during the reign of Ashurbanipal, had already secured northern Arabia's tribute status, Nabonidus managed to extend his influence much further south, thereby gaining control over some of the most lucrative trade routes in the Near East, those concerned with spices, incense and other unguents, and gold. By culling the herds of the nomadic population and policing their wells, Nabonidus forced them to become settled and thereby more easily controlled. However, once these goals were achieved, and it was not too difficult a task thanks to the fragmented nature of local polities, the king's decision to remain there longer must have been based on other motives. According to some scholars his determination to propagate Sin as the chief deity of the Babylonian pantheon had made it expedient to remove the king from the proximity of the conservative milieu of the capital. During his absence he handed over the administration of Babylonia to his son Belshazzar who thus acted *de facto* as a co-regent. The latter seems to have used his position to reverse some of the religious reform instigated by his father which aimed to diminish the status of Marduk in Babylon. In Teima, Nabonidus had greater freedom to pursue his own devotion, but he also greatly expanded the city and built palaces and temples. After ten years he returned to Babylon, duly celebrated the new New Year Festival and then completed the project closest to his heart, the new building of the Sin temple at Harran.

By this time, the Achaemenid Persians under their king Cyrus had succeeded in ousting the Medes and it was only a matter of time before they would direct their activities against Babylonia. Nabonidus prepared for this event by ordering the statues of Babylonian deities who resided in more vulnerable cities, notably Uruk, Kish and Marad, to be brought to safety to the capital. But just as the last gods entered Babylon, the Persians had penetrated into northern Babylonia. The Persians gained victory in a battle between the two armies that was fought near Opis. Soon after Sippar surrendered without bloodshed and then the Persian army entered Babylon itself, on 29 October 539, without encountering any resistance. It appears that Nabonidus was taken into exile somewhere in Iran and according to a gloss in Berossos he outlived both Cyrus and the Persian king's successor, Cambyses.

The question as to why the citizens of Babylon were so well disposed towards the new Persian ruler has been answered many times on religious grounds. It is assumed that the followers of Marduk resented the king's undisguised preference for the moon god – in his last royal inscriptions the 'Shining Crescent' of Sin regularly replaced Marduk as chief god. This would certainly have alarmed the priesthood of Esagila. There is also another aspect, that of the defence of the city's financial and economic self-interest.[34] The wealthy elite of the city decided that they would fare better under Achaemenid rule than under an anti-Babylonian native ruler such as Nabonidus. On the other hand the Persian conqueror was certainly not received as wholeheartedly as his propagandistic inscriptions suggest. He made great efforts to legitimise his rule by adopting the ancient titles and rituals of Babylonian monarchy, including the celebration of the New Year Festival.[35] He also made skilful use of the religious argument that characterised Nabonidus' preference for the moon god as a sinful act punished by Marduk who conferred kingship on Cyrus, so that he could fulfil the imperial mandate as a successor to the great kings of Assyria and Babylonia. Still, there were some uprisings in Babylonia, with two native claimants to the Babylonian throne assuming the name Nebuchadnezzar, but these were quickly squashed by the Persian authorities. The Achaemenid rulers did not become assimilated to

Babylonian culture in the way that the Amorites or the Kassites had done. In fact, while accepting to play the ritual role appropriate to the different forms of kingship within their empire, they maintained a separate cultural identity and ruled from an Iranian capital. They also did not impose their religious practices or social customs on the peoples they ruled. Hence life in Babylonia continued along familiar lines: business in Babylon and the other main urban centres such as Sippar and Uruk flourished, the cult of the ancient gods was maintained, and while much of the state business was also conducted in Aramaic, cuneiform sources remain plentiful. The country enjoyed economic stability, as the business documents from some of the wealthy private estates testify. Despite the political marginalisation of Babylonia as one of many provinces in an empire which much exceeded the limits of any previous state, it retained its prestige as a place of learning and commerce, a multi-cultural metropolis where Greeks and Persians, Jews and Syrians had settled amongst the various Babylonian groups. This state of affairs did not change significantly even after the demise of the Achaemenid empire which was brought about by the rapid conquests of Alexander the Great (356–321). According to some Greek sources he had even considered making Babylon the capital of his world empire but his premature death interrupted his ambitious plans. When his territories were divided up between his Macedonian generals, Mesopotamia was briefly administered by Perdiccas who was soon murdered (in 321) and Seleucus took his place as satrap of Babylonia, only to be dislodged by Antigonus Monophthalmos (321–301). The wars between Seleucus and Antigonus were bitterly fought and brought considerable hardship to the local population. In the end Seleucus, now named Seleucus Nikator (305–272), emerged victorious and extended his realm to include the previous satrapy of Syria and much of Anatolia.

The Macedonian rulers of Babylonia were less tolerant and respectful of local culture than their Persian predecessors. Seleucus emphasised the notion that a new time had begun by introducing a new dating system, the era of the Selucids, which began on 3 April 311. He also preferred to distance himself physically and founded a new Greek *polis,* Seleucia, on the Tigris, which reduced the status of Babylon once again, although the city remained more populous than the new foundations for a long .time.

Subsequent wars were fought over Syrian territories between the Ptolomaic rulers of Egypt and the Seleucids, but Babylonia remained little touched by these conflicts. Life in the old cities continued and although the Macedonian settlers preferred to live in their own newly built cities, business opportunities were better in the established urban centres. Even more than before, Babylonian identity was shaped by participation in the life of the Babylonian urban society, with all its opportunities for commerce and scholarly activity, religious worship and physical indulgence, with its architectural monuments that proclaimed the antiquity of its civilisation as well as the latest fashions of the new world, such as the Greek theatre and other Hellenistic amenities provided by the Seleucid kings. The last cuneiform records come from one of the oldest Mesopotamian cities, Uruk. Most of the documents from this period concern slave sales, sales of land and of temple offices, the last an apparently highly lucrative form of capital investment.[36] However, when the Greek authorities decided to tax such activities, beginning initially with the sale of slaves, the temple administration was no longer in charge of recording such transfers and the new records were written on more perishable materials such as papyrus. Babylonian was no longer spoken in daily use, and cuneiform learning became increasingly specialised to deal with astronomical matters and divination. Those who practised these arts were known to the West as Chaldeans, magicians and astrologers, who belonged to a few prominent families of scribes. The last cuneiform tablets date to the first century AD and deal with astronomical observations.

The final chapter in the history of Babylonia is marked by two apparently contradictory developments: the relatively short imperial phase from 604 to 539 when Babylonia, in the wake of Assyrian collapse, was the foremost power in the Ancient Near East; and the much longer period after its abdication from the political scene as a province of new states, first the Achaemenid empire, and then the Seleucid kingdom. Although many standard works on Babylonian history mark the death of Darius III in 330 as the end of Ancient Near Eastern history, there was no perceptible sudden end to Babylonian society. On the contrary, the Macedonian rulers, like their Persian predecessors, respected Babylonian religious institutions and continued to use the time-honoured titles of Babylonian royalty. Gradually, however, as the centre of gravity shifted to the west due to the incorporation of Syria within the Roman empire, Mesopotamia became remote from the new world, especially when continuous fighting between Rome and the Parthians made the region too marginal for commerce and trade. Although the Romans incorporated parts of Babylonia into the province of Mesopotamia which was lost only in the third century AD when the Persian Sassanians overthrew the Roman supremacy, it had lost its economic and cultural importance even though in some centres, like at Uruk for instance, Babylonian scholars continued to observe the movements of stars and planets and record their position on cuneiform diaries. But with the weakening of Roman power, the success of Christianity and the rise of a new Persian dynasty, the ancient cities became depopulated and the neglect of canals and irrigation works made much of the region infertile. It was only after some 400 years, after the triumph of the Islamic Arabs, that Mesopotamia began to revive but by then Babylonia was buried under the sands.

3

SOCIETY AND ECONOMY

A people without a king (is like) sheep without a shepherd.
A people without a foreman (is like) water without a canal inspector.
Labourers without a supervisor (are like) a field without a ploughman.
A house without an owner (is like) a woman without a husband.[1]

Despite the huge number of administrative and legal documents that have been discovered in Babylonian sites, a real understanding of the social complexity remains impossible. First of all, the cuneiform records pertain to particular institutions, especially temples and palaces, and sometimes large private business enterprises, where the exigencies of bureaucracy determined what types of transaction should be filed. The tablets refer to a multitude of persons, types of services and obligations, but they do not furnish descriptive accounts as to how the organisation operated. Efficient bookkeeping implies that only data salient for administrative purposes should be written up. This practice results in predictably formulaic and terse wording and hides all information which would have been furnished by the context. The cuneiform sources generally are unevenly distributed in time and space, thus skewing the evidence. Since the keeping of written records was a sign of political and economic stability, there were times, sometimes hundreds of years, when there was hardly any scribal activity. In addition the archaeological retrieval of any cuneiform archives is never complete. For instance, one of the best-documented Old Babylonian cities is Sippar, but most of the tablets come from the Shamash temple and the associated 'cloister' while there are no records at all from the economically very important merchant quarter. The private sector of society is usually underrepresented unless it is concerned with

70

very wealthy families who kept their own archives.[2] The rural communities, and particularly the tribally organised pastoralists, were rarely subject to bureaucratic control.

Other written sources such as literary texts (myths, epics and 'wisdom texts' such as proverbs) throw some light on aspects of social life but owing to the inherently conservative nature of Mesopotamian literature, it is difficult to locate the customs and practices alluded to, in any specific period or place.

However, while bearing in mind the limitations of the cuneiform evidence, it is probably more representative than is often thought since a significant proportion of the urban society had more or less permanent and intimate connections with the large institutions that kept records. The interpretation of these sources, however, remains speculative. Particularly difficult to study is the question of social change. Some scholars see Mesopotamian society, across the three thousand years of its history, as having changed but little, while others see it undergoing profound social upheavals and transformations. The ideological background of Assyriologists also often marks their views and perspectives. European and American scholars have given relatively more attention to the study of economics and society, and produced works on private enterprise and elite households. Some have even tried to detect evidence for the cultural importance of a professional 'middle class'.[3] Their eastern European and Soviet colleagues did their research within a Marxist framework and focused on a description of Mesopotamian society which dealt with class boundaries and the control over the means of production.[4] Such differences in outlook and theoretical models have sometimes resulted in strongly contrasting interpretations of the same body of evidence. Therefore the discussion of social structure and social change must remain tentative and provisional, based – as it has to be – on occasionally plentiful but always opaque primary sources and the limitations imposed by the intellectual habits of our own times and societies.

KINSHIP AND FAMILIES

In the Babylonian administrative and legal texts, individuals or groups were identified in a variety of ways: by kinship terms, patronymics, professional titles, by reference to organisations, and so on. The social terminology was surprisingly limited and vague, and some terms such as 'house' or 'son' could have a whole range of different meanings dependent on the context. For instance, the word *bitum* (Sumerian é) , meaning 'house', was applied to sedentary and nomadic groups alike. It could refer to a nuclear household, composed of a married couple and their young children plus any livestock and slaves, as well as to extended families uniting several generations and even to clans and tribes (for instance, the Bit Yakin of southern Babylonia). In the cuneiform texts such a 'house' is usually defined by the name of a (male) person as its titular and ancestral head. In an urban context, large institutions too were classified as 'houses'; temple estates were also seen as households of particular gods, while the palace was the household of the king. In addition, there were a number of special establishments that dealt with particular economic activities, such as weaving, livestock raising, handicrafts, etc., which were also described as 'houses'. The cuneiform sources do not differentiate between types of household into, say, private and public households,[5] urban and non-urban, large or small, between economic, social or architectural contexts.

It is difficult even to define the basic constituent of Babylonian society – was it the nuclear family, or the lineage, or even the individual, who would be associated to a number of socio-economic entities and whose status could radically change within a lifetime? Was there a fundamental difference between the city and the non-urban areas? How pronounced were social changes since the Old Babylonian period?

Let's begin by looking at the Babylonian vocabulary for family relations. Kinship terminology is not very complex; there is the father *abum*, the son *marum*, the mother *ummum*, the daughter *martum*. Siblings are called *ahum* or *ahatum* 'brother' and 'sister', uncles and aunts are father's or mother's brother or sister, there are no distinct words to define lateral relations. Male relatives refer to each other as 'brothers'. There is a distinction between the family of descent and affinal relatives, who are called *emum* 'in-laws'. It is clear from this terminology that male relationships were dominant and that partilinear descent was the main form of genealogical reckoning. The lack of greater differentiation also points to larger groupings of male solidarity within common descent lines. When the father died, his property was divided equally among his sons but generally remained in the family house.[6] At certain periods, as for instance in Old Babylonian Ur, the first son received a preferential share, perhaps as a compensation for his ritual duties towards the deceased after his death – which consisted of offerings and prayers.[7] Since the division of inheritance could lead to a fragmentation of property, various measures could be taken to limit the negative effects of such a practice – mainly by joint action by the male heirs who could assign contiguous fields to one brother or opt for co-residence and the pooling of their portions. Another possibility was for one brother to buy out his siblings. Not only could fields and houses be inherited but also slaves and temple offices.[8]

A person's welfare in old age was the responsibility of his offspring and to have no surviving children would have had serious consequences. This happened not infrequently, perhaps because of generally low life expectancy. One solution which at least the better-off Babylonians could resort to was to adopt an adult who against a stipulated compensation was contractually bound to supply his adopted parents with the necessary income. The adoptee could also expect a part of the inheritance as long as he had fulfilled his obligation.[9]

Women were born into a patriarchal household, and subject to paternal control and responsibility until their marriage into another such household. Any children belonged to the husband's family but sons were responsible for the welfare of their mother when she was widowed. According to the legal texts from various periods of Babylonian history, women were first married at puberty to men in their prime.[10] If they outlived their husbands despite frequent pregnancies, women could marry again and have greater freedom of choice than the first time. The more grown-up sons women produced, the greater was their security in old age. A child-less or barren woman was obliged to permit her husband taking a secondary wife in order to produce heirs. The normal marriage pattern was monogamous. However, wealthy men, especially kings, kept secondary wives or concubines although the position of a first wife assured superiority of status over such unofficial rivals. Numerous legal cases testify that the question of inheritance in such polygamous households could lead to litigation. Since a daughter did not inherit after her father's death she was given a share of the paternal wealth in the form of a dowry when she left the household upon marriage. This dowry remained her property and could not be controlled or taken away by her husband. Some marriage contracts list the contents of dowries, which typically comprised cooking utensils (made of valuable metals for rich girls or pottery for poorer ones), furniture (especially beds, chairs and tables), eating implements, and for the really wealthy brides, slaves and silver.[11]

While the head of a 'house' assumed a position of legal responsibility for his household, he also had rights over his dependants. In cases of litigation, wives, sons and daughters could be handed over to perform services to a debtor, or even sold outright into slavery.

The patriarchal and partilinear family was the most common social grouping into which a Babylonian of any historical period would be born and brought up. The family provided the closest and most intimate social circle, and the Alewife in the Old Babylonian Gilgamesh Epic advised the grief-stricken hero to 'appreciate the child who holds your hand, let your wife enjoy herself in your lap'.[12]

To what extent the family remained constant throughout their lives varied considerably. The most intense kin loyalty operated among the tribally organised peoples who lived a semi-nomadic existence on the fringes of the Mesopotamian plains, in a manner which probably did not differ fundamentally from those of the Bedouin in the more recent past. Since we know very little about the settled communities in rural regions, they were numerous in the Neo-Babylonian period for instance, we can only assume that they too consisted of nuclear and extended families. However, rather than bowing to the supreme authority of a tribal leader, an assembly of elders decided on matters which concerned the community.

In cities the pattern was more complex because of the existence of institutional households and the different occupational groupings which allowed for alternative or supplementary social ties. In some of the wealthier urban quarters, the written documents found in the houses make it clear that most of the male members of the families who lived there belonged to similar occupational groups, like the inhabitants of the area around 'Quiet Street' at Ur for instance, who had positions at the nearby Ekishnugal temple.[13]

Any discussion of social relations and the integration of individuals also needs to take into account the factors of life expectancy and mortality rates which were so markedly different in antiquity than in the industrialised world since the nineteenth century AD. It has been shown that in classical Rome life expectancy at birth was only between 20 and 25 years.[14] This was such a low rate that the maintenance of urban populations could not be sustained even by massive rural influx. There are, as far as I am aware, no comparable figures for Babylonian cities to provide a comparison. Archaeological evidence certainly suggests a very high infant mortality, and close human contact in urban centres helped to spread diseases. Multiple births severely restrict the life expectancy of women who, as we have seen, married as soon as they reached puberty and would have given birth several times before their twentieth year, while many of the young males were subjected to back-breaking tasks of corvée work on public amenities, the maintenance of fields and gardens, and military duty. Some of the myths (to be discussed below) also suggest that the restrictions to population growth were divinely decreed so as not to disturb the peace of the gods. It could be argued, however, that the particular way in which Mesopotamian society was organised – especially the existence of large institutional households, such as those of temples and palaces – provided a greater scope for survival than the largely privately organised rural economy of ancient Rome. The documentary evidence does not suggest that, except in periods of great economic and political stress, in Babylonian society 'the orphan rather than the *pater familias* was the dominant figure' in family relations.[15]

THE TEMPLE HOUSEHOLDS

Every city had at least one major and perhaps several minor temples. Many texts stress the interdependence between human effort and divine blessing – the gods' benevolent presence within their shrines was seen to provide the basis of human prosperity and peace – but the gods too depended on human labour and sacrifices for their sustenance. Any catastrophe that befell a city was seen as the result of the gods' anger which drove them to desert their temple and city.

Temples did not just provide cult services and worship for the gods, they were foremost seen as the gods' households. Owing to the fact that Mesopotamia's economy was primarily agrarian and that the basic crop was barley grown on irrigated fields, a large proportion of fertile land was owned and worked by institutional households, such as temples and palaces. The land was worked by teams of men and oxen who ploughed and seeded a certain area with a fixed quantity of seed.[16] The yield – especially in the third millennium – could reach ten times the quantity of original seed.[17] Only large holdings had the manpower, the equipment and the administrative expertise to ensure reliable harvests and to store the surplus. How much land a temple owned and how many people were available to work on the fields and workshops depended on a number of factors, such as the status and popularity of the god or goddess whose image dwelt in the temple – whether they belonged to the great gods of the land or were minor local deities – the largesse or interference of kings, and the political importance of the city within a given time. The largest temples, such as those of Marduk in Babylon or Anu at Uruk, possessed hundreds of acres of fields and orchards, and the gods' household comprised thousands of people, while a minor deity's shrine was maintained on a much more reduced scale.

The temple archives give details about a great number of people who served such households, from cult officers in the sanctuary proper to the personnel who maintained the agricultural estates, manned the bakeries, kitchens and stables, and produced a variety of goods in the workshops (Fig. 3.1). Some farm labourers worked for the temple estates only for a certain period of time while craftsmen, on the other hand, and scribes were employed on a more permanent basis and hence they were more securely attached to the temple household. Workers received daily rations of barley, oil and beer. More senior officials were not paid in subsistence rations but were allocated a proportion of the temple land to work themselves or lease out to others or given a proportion of the daily revenue or offerings. Such prebends (Babylonian *maṣṣartum*) were paid both in accordance to the general rank of the official within the institution and in relation to the services rendered to the deity.[18] Some prebend posts could be inherited and were thus liable to fragmentation while temple land could not be divided up when it passed on to the next generation.

Figure 3.1 Neo-Babylonian cuneiform tablet, concerning the revenue of Shamash temple at Sippar. Dated to the fifteenth year of Nabonidus. (© British Museum)

The temple archives reveal that families were often employed together, women with their children worked in the food and textile production, also as singers and dancers in the cult, while men performed a whole range of duties: menial, administrative, cultic and managerial. Since the head of the household was the deity and his or her care the *raison d'être* of the temple, there was a commensality between the god and his household. A good deal of the rations which dependants received were officially taken from the god's table. What had been offered as sacrifice was carefully divided up according to rank and status and distributed among the members of the household,[19] which presumably included seasonally employed workers too. Such practices emphasise the common bond between the deity and the populace of the city, a larger number of whom thus regularly or intermittently shared the god's food and formed part of the human household of the deity. Because all citizens could be envisaged as being the 'children' of the local gods the temples also provided charitable services for the destitute, orphaned children, widows without surviving relatives, and many of those small land-owners or tenant farmers who had fallen on hard times because of crop failure or the rapacious greed of creditors. Parents, either from economic or psychological distress, also donated children to temples. Temples could give out interest-free loans and provided food and shelter for those without a household to sustain them. Such practices not only served as a form of 'social security' to the economically marginalised people but it also helped to relieve the temples from any shortage of manpower to perform essential duties.

While temples contributed significantly to the cities' economic production and employed a large part of the population, they were also at times affected by social developments which triggered adverse social conditions. Documents from Old Babylonian Ur, for instance, show that when temple offices became fragmented because they could be kept in the family and become inherited property, the temple personnel could no longer supervise all the economic tasks necessary.[20] This meant that private citizens were subcontracted to provide the temples' needs at agreed rates of return which shifted the burden from the institution to the citizens, both urban and rural, many of whom impoverished themselves in trying to keep up their obligations.

Another important aspect for the social role of Babylonian temples was the public participation in festivals and holy days when the statues of the gods were taken outside their shrines and displayed to the citizens. Each god had his own liturgical cycle of feast days and on these occasions people were given extra rations, especially roast meat, and there was music, colourful processions, a rest from the daily labouring, and general exuberance.

Since all cities had more than one temple, with some bigger and more important than others, there were thus a number of such institutions that provided the Babylonian city dweller with a wide social network and subsistence possibilities outside his kin group which engendered a more complex sense of belonging and identity. The institution of the god's household within the city allowed people a certain degree of social and economic flexibility. It could foster upward mobility through the gradual acquisition of temple offices in the course of a professional career. In case of impoverishment, temples could guarantee at least the barest survival of the urban population, while in rural regions people had to fall back on the family for support.

As far as the economic independence of temples is concerned it could be curtailed by the king. It appears that at least since the end of the third millennium onwards (during the UrIII period) there was a tendency to make temples into 'executive organs for a centralising monarchy',[21] to integrate them into a supra-regional network of production which subsidised royal investments in infrastructure, military equipment and personnel, and trade ventures. It meant that some of the surplus the temples produced, obviously above what was needed to sustain the cult, was syphoned off to be utilised elsewhere.[22] The institutional structure of temples made them convenient agents for the central authority who could thus draw on organised manpower. In return temples benefited by being freed from the costly duties of rebuilding their architectural structures and by receiving various endowments, including land and slaves,[23] as well as 'treasure' which often derived from war booty. It can be observed that the degree of royal interference – and largesse – was proportional to the strength and stability of the regime. In times when the central authority was weak, temples reverted to a greater self-sufficiency which allowed them to maintain control over their 'capital' but also left them liable for expensive repairs.

THE PALACE HOUSEHOLDS

> In former days, in far-off years when
> [The heavens] were grieved and the earth groaned at
> evening time, the gods..
> To mankind, they became appeased and granted them
> abundance...
> To guide the land and establish the peoples they appointed
> a king.
> [.].... to rule the black-headed, the many peoples.[24]

While Babylonian kingship depends heavily on much older Sumero-Akkadian notions of the king as the divinely appointed protector and leader of the 'black-headed people', it was also interpreted in new ways according to the cultural background of those who founded new dynasties. Amorite kings like Hammurabi ruled like tribal chieftains who were personally involved in all aspects of political and social control. The Kassites, while outwardly affecting to act entirely in accordance with Mesopotamian tradition, presided over fundamental social changes and greatly enlarged the economic basis of royal power while the Neo-Babylonian dynasties were heavily influenced by Assyrian monarchical ideas. These different concepts determined to some extent how far-reaching and comprehensive the executive and economic strength of kingship was at any one period. The highly personal style of the Hammurabi administration, for instance, militated against an efficient control over his large kingdom which had been a major strength of the UrIII state. In centuries of general unrest and breakdown of order the powers of kings were substantially reduced to those of a large estate while the *pax babyloniaca* under Nebuchadnezzar II brought the king not only immense fortunes but also the unprecedented control over many sectors of the economy. We have seen that the role of the temple, apart from its religious aspects, was to provide social security and employment to the urban community. Babylonian temples were fundamentally parochial in this way, even when the god worshipped there was a 'national' god (like Marduk) or 'universal' (like the sun god Shamash). Marduk was primarily the god of Babylon, Shamash of Sippar, Enlil of Nippur, Ishtar of Uruk, and so on. Although, as we have seen, temples were in most periods linked to the central authority in a form of interdependence which secured revenues of administration for the palace and subsidies and support for building maintenance for the temple, they were only intermittently completely integrated into the state apparatus.[25]

The palace, on the other hand, was the 'house of the king' (Babylonian *bit šarrim*) and its location in any particular city was the result of political expediency rather than a deep-rootedness in a locality. While some Babylonian kings saw themselves as representative of a divine order which they upheld through ritual performances, others were essentially military leaders with a religiously sanctioned remit to control and safeguard the integrity of the 'land'. New dynasties were invariably initiated by a forceful take-over of the existing royal power base and could become established only if the resistance from the major cities, anxious to retain some degree of independence over their own affairs, was successfully suppressed. The king's position towards the urban centres was often ambiguous, and any slackening of royal control could be exploited to minimise interference. The presence of a palace household in a given city, except at Babylon, was an imposition by force rather than an intrinsic constituent like the temple.

The economic activities of the state were organised in the form of separate households which were hierarchically organised and subjected to the authority of the king.[26] Although the sheer size of some palatial households could easily rival those of the largest temples, and therefore also demanded a large labour force, the personnel was differently configured because of their relationship to the king. First of all there were the members of his family and kin group who formed the inner circle who, like the Kassites, had a different ethnic and linguistic background. Then came the courtiers and officials who were directly in the king's service and formed an entourage eager to please and flatter their master. He in turn could reward them with well-remunerated offices including positions within the temple hierarchies. Courtiers could be members of the royal family but there was also a place for ambitious local urbanites, especially scribes, diviners, exorcists and physicians who could either enter the king's court on a full-time basis or serve as needed. Since the king's position depended to no small degree on his control over armed forces, his military leaders and trusted soldiers formed another important part of his court. They were generally given land for their loyalty and services rendered. The land thus handed over by some Kassite kings for instance, often vast areas, was generally outside the territory belonging to urban centres and had often been won through fighting.

The city dwellers, especially those inhabiting the old sacred cities, were generally reluctant to perform military duties, and some of the privileged cities, such as Sippar, Nippur and Babylon, were exempt from conscription. Most of the soldiers were therefore of rural and tribal origin, and had superficial if any ties to the city.

Finally there were slaves, generally people who been captured during military campaigns. Such newly recruited slaves were much less willing to perform than those domestic slaves who were born into a particular family, and needed much tighter supervision. They could be used for the construction work which kings were responsible for or sold on.

During the Old Babylonian period there was another group of palace dependants whose status was higher than that of slaves and lower than that of normal citizens. They were called *muškenum* and seem to have been used primarily for agricultural labour. It is not clear how one became a *muškenum,* whether they were pauperised citizens or recruited from recently settled tribal immigrants for instance, or coerced into providing palace services. In other periods, such services were demanded from the local population as a civic duty to their ruler.

Altogether, palace households can be characterised by the higher proportion of non-native (meaning not of the city) citizens than those of temples, and a higher degree of coercion. Palaces in times of peace and prosperity functioned like large-scale economic enterprises: apart from being agricultural holdings they also engaged in the manufacturing of goods, especially textiles and luxury items, as well as long-distance trade. As such they provided business opportunities for enterprising individuals, as well as employment for craftsmen and artisans. It has been shown that palaces, as early as the Old Babylonian period, could leave the delivery of many services – from agricultural production and the exploitation of wild resources (fishing and fowling), up to the collection of taxes – to the private agents or middlemen.[27]

In summary, palaces fulfilled a rather different role in Babylonian society than temples. Because they were officially serving the whole of the country they had a greater integrative role between individual cities and, primarily due to the military personnel, they mediated between city and countryside. They also were less socially homogenous, comprising of a sometimes foreign elite and a number of personally ambitious persons of varying background. Palaces provided employment at varying levels of remuneration or at subsistence levels, but also relied on forced labour for architectural and civic projects, such as temple repairs, the construction of city walls and irrigation works. The institution functioned best in those times just after the consolidation of power under a new dynasty, when the spoils of foreign wars flowed into the king's treasure house and when the imposed internal and external peace provided a spur to long-distance trade. In such times both local citizens and foreigners benefited from the presence of a royal household and individuals could rise to positions of influence and great wealth and there was enough silver and surplus to endow temples and allow even the poor some share of affluence. Generally though, palaces never fulfilled a charitable role. While temples would put up money to ransom prisoners of war and save them from slavery, or gave loans with low or no interest, palaces were concerned with enhancing the economic and personal power of their master, the king. The royal household was vulnerable to internal dissent and intrigue, to revolts and external aggression. Palaces and their store-houses and armouries were a prime target for a conquering army. Cities could function perfectly well without a palace and the destruction of a 'king's house' was never lamented as the destruction of a temple was. The palace remained an institution that was often imposed from without, a mixed blessing at best. Thus, we have seen that whenever Babylonia was ruled by an outside power, such as the Assyrians and later the Persians, as long as they did not interfere too obtrusively in the affairs of the cities, this was not seen as a calamity. There was no general resistance against the foreign rule as such, only a jealous defence of urban self-determination which could, however, lead to coalitions with oppressed tribal groups, as happened in the seventh century. More typically the Babylonian reaction was a readiness to compromise in order to safeguard the continuity of cherished institutions, such as the temples and the *karum*, or merchants' quarter.

THE MERCHANT COMMUNITY

> Shamash, there confronts you the caravan, those journeying in fear,
> The travelling merchant, the agent who is carrying the capital.[28]

Although much of the agricultural production and distribution, as well as manufacturing, was carried out by temples and palaces, there was also an important independent commercial sector in any Babylonian city.[29] Since the alluvial plains were fertile enough to produce a surplus of food on irrigated land, but lacking in most raw materials, especially metals, trade was of a very great importance from the earliest time. It used to be thought that overland trade and internal distribution of imported commodities were always the prerogatives of the great institutions. This may well have been the case in the early ages of Mesopotamian civilisation but during the Babylonian times much of the commercial activities were carried out by merchants.[30] Because communication within cities in the alluvial plain was generally by waterways and on boats, the commercial district which concerned itself with inter-city and long-distance trade was located near the landing quays and known as *karum:* 'harbour'.[31] It seems that this was outside rather than inside the city walls, and the *karum* had its own administrative and judicial set-up which was presided over by the 'harbour-master'. The king would raise tax revenue from trading activities but generally did not interfere in the affairs of the merchant community. Unfortunately no 'harbour' archive in Babylonia has yet been published, so details about the volume of business and the number of people involved remain unknown. According to the Old Assyrian texts from *karum* Kanesh in Anatolia, the start-up capital for trade ventures was often supplied by wealthy businessmen within the city to enterprising merchants who were attracted by the high profits to be made from exporting finished and raw textiles and tin and from importing silver.[32] Since in this case the 'harbour' was a very long way from the city of Ashur, it had considerable independence and operated as a self-sufficient community next to an Anatolian city. It is not clear to what extent the Babylonian *karum* was similarly detached and whether all or only some (foreign) merchants resided extramurally. At any rate, as an institution it had an important function for the city, since it allowed the movement of goods produced locally – Babylonia was a prime producer of luxury goods, for instance, which were in high demand across the Near East, even in Egypt – and the receipt of raw materials which were lacking in the country. On the other hand, the merchants were also agents of distribution for locally produced goods, including grain. Dealings with merchants were based largely on trust, since the measures used varied from city to city (although attempts at standardisation were made repeatedly). The following passage from a hymn to Shamash illustrates the wrong and right conduct of a merchant:

> The merchant who [practises] trickery as he holds the balances,
> Who uses two sets of weights, thus lowering the ....,

He is disappointed in the matter of profit and loses [his
capital].
The honest merchant who holds the balances [and gives]
good weight—
Everything is presented to him in good measure [...].[33]

The volume of business depended on the general state of affairs in
the country – wars and tribal unrest had a very negative impact while
stability, peace and control over long-distance trade routes were good
for business. The location and infrastructure of a city within a given
political framework were also important. While the ancient cities in
the Mesopotamian south, such as Ur, had enjoyed a huge volume of
mercantile transactions during the third and early second millennium, especially for sea-borne traffic in the Persian Gulf, by the end
of the second millennium they had become nearly deserted because
of the deterioration of the soil and a shift of the waterway that
connected with the Gulf. Since rivers in the alluvial plain were liable
to change their courses sometimes significantly, a city could temporarily lose its harbour altogether, as happened to Nippur at the
end of the Old Babylonian period. The position of Babylon on the
Euphrates, which flowed right through the city, and its function as
capital of a powerful empire, made it also the most important trade
centre during Neo-Babylonian times. Because of the paucity of
written materials about any particular *karum* little can be said as
to who the merchants and quay workers were,[34] what proportion
of them were foreigners from distant countries – they are alluded to
in literary texts – and how many were native citizens who worked
in the 'harbour' but lived within the city. It would have been in
keeping with the nature of the trade enterprise to retain a certain
flexibility and to follow the business where it could be found. There
are indications that some Babylonians were keen to explore foreign
countries themselves but the documentary evidence is scant. It
appears that most of them carried out their business activities within
Mesopotamia. The well-known voyage of an influential merchant,
attached to the Murashu and Egibi firms of the sixth century, to
southern Iran for instance, now appears to have been inspired by
diplomatic rather than mercantile considerations.[35]

The institution of the *karum* remained essentially an independent
sector of society which was to fulfil the vital function of supplying

cities with raw materials for the various branches of Babylonian manufacture as well as importing luxury items and exporting Babylonian goods. The *wakil tamkarim,* the 'head of the merchants', could liaise with either temple or palace about special commissions but was primarily answerable to his colleagues. In Old Babylonian Sippar he was responsible for the tax collected for the king.[36] In this way the city institutions could avail themselves of the merchants' services. In the Neo-Babylonian cities merchants acted as agents for temples, purchasing their agricultural produce as livestock with silver, and supplying the sanctuaries with both necessities (sacrificial sheep) as well as rare goods and precious items, such as for instance juniper resin, honey, bitumen, precious stones, gold, and so forth.[37] At times, such as in the Old Babylonian period, merchants could also be contracted with the collection of taxes for the palace, which turned the merchants into tax farmers, supplying the palace with barley and silver, and keeping the proceeds from the sale of the natural products they had access to.[38] Fundamentally, though, the *tamkarum* did not need the palace in order to function. He attached himself to a city, making use of its infrastructure, its market potential and the local businessmen's willingness to enter into mutually beneficial relationships. As a politically neutral and market-oriented institution the *karum* acted as a stabilising social force in so far as it was able to provide services for the economy without being under the direct control of the crown or the cities. In Babylonia the distribution of goods within the country and their movements from and to the outside world were so important that the self-determination of merchants was the only way to guarantee continuity. Perhaps the end of the violent rivalries between Mesopotamian cities since the mid-second millennium could be linked to growth of mercantile activities throughout the land. On the other hand, their wealth and comparative exposure beyond the protection of city walls would have made them an attractive target to marauding tribal immigrants. This was one of the reasons why those centuries that witnessed large-scale population movements from the western deserts were experienced as particularly hard for the urban population because it interfered with the flow of merchandise and raw materials. On the other hand, it could also be argued that the *karum,* poised as it was between city and country, the wider world and the local markets, was a good place to accommodate newcomers with a sense of adventure and an eye for business, who would make use of their kinship relations to obtain free passage through occupied terrain, to secure access to overland routes and to venture outwards. These were no doubt contributing factors in the growing importance of the southern tribes in the late second millennium and the Arabs in the mid-first millennium. The ability of merchants, with their loose organisation and their unique position within Babylonian society, to adapt swiftly to new circumstances – the rise and fall of dynasties, the geographical variations of the landscape, the demographic shifts – proved thus to be one of the mainstays of this civilisation.

BUSINESSMEN AND ENTREPRENEURS

We have seen that at various times in Mesopotamian history, there was more or less room for private enterprise to flourish. Since the great institutions soon realised that the regular employment of large numbers of people was costly to administer and organise, services were subcontracted to independent middlemen. So, for instance, in Old Babylonian Ur, one temple entrusted the provision of bread to the temple to individuals who subcontracted independent bakers with the production and delivery.[39] Agricultural labours were more profitably organised by employing people only for a set time and for particular tasks while the rest of the year they worked their own land. Revenues could also be collected from people who were contractually bound to deliver an agreed proportion of their yield to the institution which owned the land while they could keep the rest. Such an arrangement worked well for the producers in good years; in bad times the institution would still be assured of its share but the risk was borne by the farmer or herdsman who had to find the means to maintain his obligations. This could often be met only by taking out loans, in silver or in kind, from individuals who demanded interest for such services. Institutions, even temples, also engaged in the lucrative business of lending, or usury.[40]

Crucial for the development of such early banking services and the practice of usury was the introduction of silver (and later gold) as a means of payment. As early as 2500 silver had become 'the primary definition of economic value' although it was not issued as coins but in weight, carried in different shapes, such as rings or rods.[41] However, barley could also function as a form of cheap money and could be lent out. After all many people's basic wages were paid in cereals and beer (as well as sesame oil). Most loans were for a short period of time, like a few months, or until the harvest was in. Some loans were made without interest but rates charged were between 20 and 33 per cent.[42] Moneyed individuals would lend silver for a variety of purposes, not just to meet obligations of repayment but also to finance a variety of business ventures.

One citizen of Old Babylonian Ur, for instance, called Dumuzi-gamil,[43] began by borrowing 500 g of silver from wealthy merchants with a partner, at the rate of 23.9 per cent, for a period of five years. This start-up capital allowed him to engage in a variety of business activities, such as providing bread for the Nanna temple, lending out money himself, as well as acting as an agent to the lending section of the Nanna temple. He had several different partners and contacts with different sectors of the Ur society, the temple, the merchants, and the palace who also depended on him for the provision of bread and possibly meat. We see from this example that the system worked well as an investment of surplus capital by moneyed individuals who did not wish to engage personally in time-consuming and risky business. By making substantial loans of nearly 30 per cent they almost trebled their initial outlay within the five years. For Dumuzi-gamil the different activities he could start up with the advanced money provided him with a good income. He and his colleagues were able to exploit an economic niche created by the institutional practice of subcontracting managerial services.

Businessmen also took on the supervision of agricultural services, collected their produce, and marketed them. Then they paid the agreed amount to the institution and kept the rest as profit. Since the maximisation of returns was their main means of achieving profit they would squeeze from the primary producers as much return as possible. The archives show that they also tried to slow down the payments to the institutions which had given them vast amounts of silver. This could be invested further in usurious loans. Such 'capitalist' practices contributed not only to the environmental pressure on the agricultural land as farmers and pastoralists were forced to increase their production, but also to the impoverishment of the farming population. More and more small-holders and agricultural workers lost control over their means of production by having to sell their fields, boats, livestock and so on and to enter into a serf-like dependency on their creditors. However, since such forms of private enterprise were so intimately linked to the palace and temple institutions it was easily affected by political change. The fortunes of the Old Babylonian Ur business community began to wane when the palace took control over the resource management and greatly curbed the independence of the temple estates. Merchants rather than local businessmen were then entrusted with the collection of taxes and rents. When the central administration moved north to Larsa and rebellions in the south were violently repressed, the whole region became marginal and lost its economic importance.

The interdependence between private management and large institutions proved too useful for both parties for it to be restricted to a particular period in time although we do not always have the archival evidence. During the first millennium, such contractual arrangements were made between temples and businessmen, as documented at Sippar and Uruk.[44] Some archives from the sixth century on the other hand show that the by then increasingly important sector of small-holding farmers availed themselves of independent middlemen to market their produce in the urban centres. A certain Iddin-Marduk, for instance, made his fortune by transporting rurally grown onions to the town of Borsippa.[45] He then extended his activities to engage in short-term loans for his producers and royal commissions.

At this stage the difference between merchants and businessmen became blurred as both were engaged in money-lending as well as buying and selling commodities. During the Late Babylonian period, when the country was under Persian rule, mercantile activities became even more diversified. Several archives belonging to wealthy families have been discovered which detail their business affairs for generations. At this time too, the Persian court decided to contract the administration of large areas to local entrepreneurs, such as the region around Nippur for instance, which was run by the Murashu firm.[46] The Persian administration benefited in the same way as the Babylonian institutions – they were sure of a regular income but unburdened by the task of managing workmen, middlemen and so on. Here too though, changes in the overall administration and the control of resources could terminate such mutually advantageous relationships.

Generally the Babylonian businessmen provided an interface between the great institutions, especially forms of state administration, and the primary producers, and made a living by providing services to a large sector of the population. At periods when these services were seen as most indispensable their influence was greatest, which led to considerable exploitation of the primary, mainly agricultural producers.

Detailed studies of the documentary evidence show that especially in the Neo-Babylonian period, private contractors or middlemen also took on land which the palace had assigned to particular ethnic or vocational groups in return for services and obligations. The entrepreneurs could make the agricultural exploitation more profitable by providing four-oxen teams.[47]

The archives also demonstrate that anyone with a good sense for business and good communication skills, who could make and maintain contacts with a great variety of peoples and was willing to put much effort into the business, could prosper. Provided they could raise some start-up capital and did well in the first venture, they could build up a flourishing business in a relatively short time. One did not need inherited money or estates; slaves too could become entrepreneurs.[48] Once a substantial business had been established, and the general political and economic conditions were favourable, then sons would enter the firm and eventually take over the enterprise to form such large and well-connected companies like the Egibi or Murashu houses which could then limit competition by smaller firms or individual businessmen.

In Old Babylonian Ur, a lot of entrepreneurs lived in a particular part of the city and they maintained close contact with each other and intermarried.[49]

Women were often involved in business partnerships although the absence of gender designations in some documents makes this less obvious. They could help their husbands or carry on the business after his demise, but they could also act independently and finance their own enterprise.[50] One type of business activity in which women seem to have been especially well represented was the keeping of taverns and the brewing of beer. Such places could be made even more profitable by offering female companionship. In the Late Babylonian period even such services were commercialised and under the control of large firms, such as the Egibi, who employed a large number of women in the brewing processes and the 'entertainment business' of taverns.[51] Prostitution of course was an even older private enterprise in which women could engage, especially in the large cities. The blessings and curses which Enkidu directs at the Harlot in the Epic of Gilgamesh reflect both the harshness of such an existence as well as its rich rewards.

The example of the Babylonian businessmen (and women) shows that there was a good deal of flexibility in the social fabric which allowed a whole range of people from different backgrounds to make a living and even considerably enrich themselves by providing a range of services – managerial, administrative and financial – by acting as middlemen between different institutions and private persons. We have also seen, however, that during times when such business opportunities were particularly lucrative, it also had a negative effect on the producers at the base who found themselves squeezed into overproduction and eventual loss of their independence. The following lines, again from the Shamash hymn, deal with the morals of businessmen:

> The merchant who practises trickery as he holds the corn measure,
> Who weighs out loans (or corn) by the minimum standard, but requires a large quantity in repayment,
> the curse of the people will overtake him before his time,
> If he demanded repayment before the agreed date, there will be guilt before him.
> His heir will not assume control of his property,
> Nor will his brothers take over his estate.
> The honest merchant who weighs out loans (of corn) by the maximum standard,
> thus multiplying kindness,
> is pleasing to Shamash, and he will prolong his life.
> He will enlarge his family, gain wealth,
> And like the water of a never failing spring [his] descendants will never fail.[52]

SCRIBES AND INTELLECTUALS

While the merchants typically operated beyond the boundaries of state and city – mediating between the Babylonian urban and rural world and 'the four quarters of the universe', by controlling the flow of vital material goods – and the businessmen inserted themselves into the social fabric to expand markets, scribes could operate only within an urban context and as providers of traditional expertise.

They were employed by all the social sectors just discussed – the temples, palaces (or royal offices generally) and the *karum*, as well as the wealthy business elite. Their main purpose was to guarantee the smooth operation of bureaucratic control, to record transactions, keep accounts, write up contracts and legal decisions, and to maintain the system of cuneiform education. Of comparatively minor importance, although of much greater interest to subsequent generations, was their creative role, either transmitting an oral and written literary tradition, or inventing new works, such as hymns and epics, wisdom texts and those concerned with royal proclamations. Most revered in ancient times were those scribes skilled in the esoteric arts of divination and the mastery of magic.

The complexity of the writing system, as well as the many different professional specialisations, meant that such training had to be learned in a school – in a systematic and time-consuming way, not just passed on from generation to generation by current practitioners.[53] The education of scribes proceeded in several stages. First, pupils had to master the repertoire of cuneiform signs with the help of special lists that taught the syllables. Next came Akkadian personal names, lexical lists and proverbs. Once the students had mastered the rudiments of writing they practised writing letters, contracts and accounts. In the Late Babylonian period, students also learned to write proverbs as well as literary and historical texts. Mathematical instructions, such as the use of different measuring systems, field surveying and calculations of different kinds, were also taught at the secondary level. Such formation made it possible to operate as a clerk in the different institutions for general administrative duties. Higher-level training involved the writing and reading of literary texts, in the Old Babylonian period also of Sumerian examples, and the bilingual lexical lists. In the late period students acquired a knowledge of the classical texts of Babylonian culture (such as the Creation Epic, wisdom literature, religious texts, and the more sophisticated lexical lists, such as synonym lists), as well as the first stages of the diviner's arts. In order to achieve the highest grades of learning and to conclude a professional training – such as *ašipu* (incantation specialist and physician), *baru* (omen interpreter), *kalu* (cult singer) and *tupšar enuma anu enlil* (astronomers) – students had to undergo an apprenticeship with such professionals, who made specialist literature available and provided the essential oral exegesis.[54] The most learned and diplomatically skilled could look towards employment at the royal court. Especially the Assyrian monarchs of the seventh century, such as Esarhaddon and Ashurbanipal, had an entourage of top-grade 'scholars' whose expertise in detecting and averting potential evil from king and country was a matter of national security. In the late first millennium some scribes trained in cuneiform could also write in Aramaic and Greek, as some tablets with interlinear glosses show. A highly educated specialist would receive twenty or even fifty times the remuneration paid to ordinary clerks who were paid the same rations as craftsmen.

The rate of literacy varied from time to time, depending on the needs of the institutions for the administrative personnel and the general prosperity. It appears that it was highest during the Old Babylonian period, to support the complex bureaucratic structures, and was lowest in the so-called dark ages, when economic and political turmoil severely disrupted civil life. Scribes were much more intimately linked to the great institutions such as the palace and the temples than were the merchants who could carry out their professions without their involvement in state or temple contexts. While some scribes could function independently, for instance as freelance letter writers, or at a higher level, as diviners, most were employed, either full-time or part-time, by a state-run office or attached to a temple or a wealthy private firm.

Towards the end of the first millennium, alphabetic systems which could be learned much more easily, such as Aramaic and later Greek, came more and more in use, and cuneiform was retained only in the traditional centres of learning such as Babylon and Uruk. At that period, when the political independence had long been lost, and a new civilisation began to exert its influence, the cultural value of the old Mesopotamian writing acquired great prestige, as a precious link to the past and the basis of a separate identity; it also presented new employment opportunities.[55] It is therefore not surprising to find that scribes of the late period belonged to a few families or clans of literary ancestors and enjoyed a high prestige at least in those circles which held traditional learning in high esteem. At that time too we find the practice of leaving school tablets and other tablets as votive offerings to the Babylonian gods, asking that they accept them and grant 'health and long life, for a healthy offspring, and (intellectual) understanding'.[56]

Babylonian intellectuals and scribes made an important contribution to their society by preserving and transmitting to future generations some of the core values of Mesopotamian culture which gave it such extraordinary resilience and longevity. However, their role was not merely reproductive and conservative, since each generation adapted the transmitted knowledge to suit their own times. Certain notions disappeared and with them whole literary genres, while others came to the fore. The literate elite also had to respond to new political leaders and their often rather different concepts of sovereignty which perhaps could have had a more detrimental effect on the urban culture had it not been for their mediating role. New kings were made familiar with the cautionary tales of previous rulers, for instance, as well as with examples of what had made them great. Since the scribes were the treasurers of the past they could impress upon their masters the necessity to conform to the traditional values of Mesopotamian kingship, to respect its traditions and behave 'like a Sargon' and to curry the favour of the gods without whose assistance no king had ever ruled successfully. This seems to have worked especially well in the Old Babylonian period when the uncultivated tribal leaders 'fresh from the desert' assumed the thrones of Babylon, or during the rule of the Kassite kings. To the population at large, the scribes represented authority, both of the institutions they served, and of transmitted knowledge of past generations. Since they did not occupy a fixed place in a rigid social system, as say the mandarins in Confucian China, they did not represent a class. They could be poor, some were slaves and trained at the temple for instance, or very well off.[57] The majority of scribes at a palace or a temple were working for subsistence rations, the same as other artisans, while a few attained the status of courtiers or high-ranking temple officials and priests and became very wealthy. This more or less even distribution among the different social strata of Babylonian cities, without enjoying specific privileges, accounts for some of the social solidarity and insights into the lives of ordinary people which mark some genres of cuneiform writing, but it also meant that they permeated society and perhaps acted as a leaven, distributing certain traditional values such as the respect for learning across a much wider population. In this respect they seem to have occupied a similar place to those purveyors of oral tradition in other parts of the world, such as the *griots* of sub-Saharan Africa for instance. They based their view of the world on a wider and deeper base than their illiterate contemporaries and were thus in a better position to interpret the present and adapt to change. Like the merchants who travelled beyond the plains of Mesopotamia and who were mediating between city and country, far and near, the scribes and intellectuals mediated between the past and future, low and high, and thus contributed to the richness and vitality of Babylonian culture.

SOCIAL DIVISION AND COHESION

The palace and the temples were theoretically bound to safeguard the subsistence of their indentured labourers but, as has been shown, the burden of maintaining a large workforce at all times was often too onerous. Furthermore, by levying taxes and rents on any kind of income, and by exacting forced labour and military services, the palace generally exploited the urban as well as the rural population. The privileges of freedom from taxes and military duty, which some cities enjoyed, were therefore a great boon. Even the temples, although they had a more charitable agenda towards the population of their locality, could monopolise production and create a heavy dependency which provided them with a steady income at no great expense. Altogether, there were considerable inequalities in the degree of independence, freedom, and economic and social status. While we have seen that there was no class system in Babylonia, and that slaves could achieve high degrees of learning and become wealthy, there were sharp differences between the indentured and dependent workforce who laboured in fields and workshops for subsistence rations, and those who enjoyed a safe income from lucrative prebends or who had independent means of income, like the merchants and businessmen. During the centuries of Assyrian domination, the educated and urban elite, known as *mare ali* (literally 'sons of the city'), were given considerable political and economic advantages over other parts of the population, especially the tribal immigrants. The Assyrian masters wanted to encourage greater solidarity, at least between the intelligentsia of both countries, in order to reduce the chances of violent rebellion in the south.[58] While the ideology envisaged a world order where it was the lot of all mankind to submit to heavy work and which justified unequal access to resources as a managerial solution to complexity (as the proverb quoted at the beginning of this chapter shows), it is clear that people did not submit for ever to prolonged and unjust exploitation of the common people. A number of texts emphasise the idea of justice and social responsibility, especially of the ruler towards his subjects. Historical records testify to rebellions and uprisings, where subjugated cities rose against suppression by unpopular regimes.

Especially revealing for the relationship between conscripted workers and their masters is the account of an Old Babylonian Flood story, known after its protagonist as Atrahasis.[59] The action is set in primordial times before mankind had been created. The gods had to do all the work themselves but one group of gods, called the Anunnaki, imposed the whole workload on another group of gods, the Igigi, and thereby established an unjust and unequal distribution of labour.

> The gods had to dig out canals,
> had to clear channels, the lifelines of the land,
> (.....)
> they groaned and blamed each other,
> grumbled over the masses of excavated soil:
> 'Let us confront our [ ] the chamberlain,
> And get him to relieve us from our hard work.'

The Igigi were given the back-breaking task of clearing canals and rivers, the sort of work that the king could exact from the populace as forced labour. The subjugated deities bear this, albeit grudgingly, for some time but then they embark on a violent protest, setting fire to their tools and surrounding the dwelling of Ellil, the leader of the celestial gods. Ellil assembles the other great gods and sends a delegation to hear the complaint of the Igigi who send the following answer to his question as to who is in charge of the fighting and who had declared war:

> Every single one of us gods declared war!
> We have put [a stop] to the digging,
> the load is excessive, it is killing us!
> Our work is too hard, the trouble too much!
> So every single one of us gods
> Has agreed to complain to Ellil.

This message is duly heard by the great gods and they acknowledge that they were well aware of the dissatisfaction among the oppressed workers but they were content to wait until it proved unbearable and the 'rabble' revolted. The solution was to substitute one group of exploited labourers for another. The Igigi, being gods, are henceforth freed from forced labour which is imposed on mankind, specially created for the purpose from the blood of a murdered god, mixed with clay. The 'industrial action' of the oppressed gods led to their liberation from imposed work. We have no direct records that people rebelled in a similar way but in another wisdom text we also find warnings against abuse of power:

> If a king does not heed justice, his people will be
> thrown into chaos, and his land will be devastated.[60]

Any heterogeneous society, especially if it has pronounced differences in people's standard of living, needs integrative measures to bind the different sectors together. In Babylonia, the city population had its local deities who to some extent marked the identity of a place. Furthermore, the frequent and periodic festivals and holy days which the temple organised brought relief from daily drudgery and were the occasion to distribute food stuffs and beer. The royal courts also put on displays, especially after victorious campaigns abroad, when booty was shown and some of it deposited in the temple treasuries. Other civic amenities, such as public squares and taverns, were meeting places for locals and strangers alike, as were the markets and the *karum*. Even forced labour, such as the clearing of irrigation canals and the participation in public building projects, especially the renovation of temples, must have had some integrative effect by the experience of a shared burden.

It was much more difficult to unite the whole country, all the different cities which jealously guarded their privileges, and the rural areas which were inhabited by many different groups of people, some settled there for many generations, others still practising a semi-nomadic form of living. After the mid-first millennium there was the added problem of the displaced foreign groups who had been 'cleansed' and resettled from their homeland for political reasons. At that time there was not even a commonly spoken language, since Babylonian was used only among certain groups in the old cities, although Aramaic served as a general medium of communication, especially during the Achaemenid period. An age-old solution to the problem of how to absorb and enculture newcomers, whether they be resettled communities or tribal groups, was to assign them land against certain obligations.[61] This gave people a place they could call their own and which provided a relatively secure subsistence base. It also induced a new attitude both to the land and to the dominant culture that had thus made room for them. To what extent people were aware of sharing a common culture is equally problematic because of the one-sided nature of texts which were produced in an urban milieu. To foster a 'national' consciousness was hardly a goal for the ancient rulers, but the royal inscriptions and other texts refer to the problems that arose precisely because there was little common ground between a highly educated priest in Uruk and a Sutean tribesman. To some extent foreign aggression helps to coalesce the population into some form of unity and it seems that the Elamite invasions in the mid-second and the Assyrian wars of the seventh century did have such an effect, as we see from the coalitions which united very diverse groups in a common effort to drive out the enemy. Just as some immigrant groups were absorbed by making them settle on arable land, others who were perhaps less ready for the shift to sedentary life were incorporated into the army and tied more to the persona of the king, who eventually could reward them for long service with land. This can be clearly observed in all Babylonian periods.

The civic festivals of the period, especially the New Year Festival, in essence remained a local celebration of the city of Babylon, although it contained elements which made it more inclusive, such as the assembly of the gods from other cities. The recitation of the Creation Epic lays claim that the whole universe was ritually re-created on such occasions but it is doubtful whether this had an echo much beyond the ritual space where it was performed.

Babylonian society obviously underwent profound changes throughout its nearly two-thousand-year-long history and there was no consistent ethnic or linguistic unity at any one period. The only continuities which can be discerned are the main social units of kinship and the great institutions. The temples in particular ensured the transmission of cultural norms which maintained links to the distant past. The temple and palace households, primarily charged with the bulk of economic production, also provided opportunities for independent enterprise as well as ensuring the subsistence of the urban masses. The intellectual and moral outlook of a large number of people was therefore shaped by the participation in large-scale institutions whose ideological basis was formulated and sustained by a literate elite.

4

RELIGION

Every day worship your god.
Sacrifice and benediction are the proper accompaniment of incense.
Present your free-will offering to your god,
For this is proper toward the gods.
Prayers, supplication, and prostration
Offer him daily, and you will get your reward.
Then you will have full communion with your god.
In your wisdom study the tablet.
Reverence begets favour,
Sacrifice prolongs life,
And prayer atones for guilt.
He who fears the gods is not slighted by .[..]
He who fears the Anunnaki extends [his days].[1]

He who waits on his god has a protecting angel,
The humble man who fears his goddess accumulates wealth.[2]

I have made my effort. Now let an increase in wealth, flocks, divine favour –
things for which I have prayed to Marduk, come about.
May I experience divine favour,
and may he who is granted it live long.[3]

Religious practices and beliefs in any society cannot be simply summarised or brought to a common denominator because of the very personal nature of people's attitudes which may change as a person matures, quite apart from the different degrees of their involvement in religious rituals or observances. A literate, full-time temple officiant would have an infinitely more detailed knowledge of the liturgical procedures and the right formulae than an ordinary householder. People's inner convictions or sense of piety are difficult to express and research even in contemporary societies; for a long-vanished culture, such as that of the Babylonians, it is quite impossible. Leo Oppenheim once wrote that 'an account of Mesopotamian religion should not be written'.[4] He warned that despite the great number of tablets discovered among the ruins of temples and in the royal libraries, and the rich archaeological record of apparently sacred buildings, as well as the iconography on seals and other artefacts, 'the mechanics and functioning, and the meanings which motivated the enactments of the cult, remain removed from us as if pertaining to another dimension'.[5]

Recognising that we can neither grasp the deeply private emotional responses of individuals, nor penetrate the arcane meanings which certain rituals had for their trained performers, we can nevertheless try to delineate which options were available to the Babylonians when it came to their dealings with those aspects of human existence that remain forever problematic – death and suffering and the sheer unpredictability of life.

BABYLONIAN GODS AND GODDESSES

Mesopotamian religion in all its complexity developed over millennia. The lexical lists record the names of many hundreds of gods and goddesses, many of whom are quite unknown from any other textual sources. Like in all polytheistic systems gods did not become obsolete even when they were no longer actively worshipped in any particular temple. Likewise the gods of immigrants and conquerors found a place in the crowded world of divine forces. People's names, which were generally composed like miniature prayers addressing a particular god, give valuable clues to the popularity and currency of deities during certain periods; given that so many names of individuals were recorded in the administrative texts, such prosopographic data are very revealing for the heterogeneity of religious loyalties. Most other texts which concern religion were either composed in the temples, and therefore concern mainly the deities who resided there, or by highly trained scribes in the service of kings. Since the legitimacy of a Babylonian ruler was seen to depend on divine approval it was important to underline royal devotion, especially to those gods who were traditionally associated with sovereignty, and to those whose temples were powerful institutions at the time. Many of the texts composed for royal rituals lay great emphasis on the state-like organisation of the pantheon which had a clearly defined hierarchy and areas of responsibility like those of ministers. Owing to the conservative nature of Mesopotamian scholarly tradition, there was comparatively little change as to which deities constituted the inner circle of power. The most important were the sky-god Anu, whose epithet 'father of the gods' points to seniority and overall command; the master-magician and god of wisdom Ea (associated with the underground waters); the 'executive manager' Ellil who presided over the divine assembly and conferred kingship; and the goddess of love and war, Ishtar. Already in the Old Babylonian period the previously little-known Marduk became strongly associated with Babylonian kings and eventually, certainly by the end of the second millennium, had taken over most of the epithets and functions of Ellil and even some authority hitherto ascribed to Anu. Such far-reaching changes in the official theological structure needed to be explained by new or edited older narratives which were officially recited on important state occasions, such as the New Year celebrations. The rise of Marduk is described at length in the *enuma elish*[6] a composition that combines older cosmogonic myths with the enumeration of the hundred names of Marduk. His unrivalled position as leader of the gods is based on his prowess as their champion who defeats the forces of primeval chaos and inertia. In this respect he resembles a king who wins power by strength and perseverance rather than a representation of a force of nature. The official Babylonian pantheon reflects the ideological position of any given period but should not be taken as representative for Babylonian religion. It may be more fruitful to compare their notions of the supernatural world to that of their cities; contained yet crowded, highly institutionalised yet with enough room for individual enterprise because of the existence of several institutions, hierarchical in terms of political control and yet operating on the basis of consensus. There are many references, for instance, to assemblies and corporate groups of gods, such as the Igigi or Annunaki who in the myths appear both as executives of higher command and as powerful forces of dissent.[7]

Babylonian gods do not dwell outside cities, there are no mountains for them to sit on as in Syria–Palestine, there are no arcadian glades as in Greece or grottoes and disappearing rivers as in Anatolia. Even when deities are directly related to astral phenomena (Shamash the sun, Sin the moon, Ishtar Venus, and so on) they always have a fixed abode on earth in a particular city. Thus Inanna-Ishtar was the goddess of Uruk, Sin the moon god resided at Ur, Shamash the sun god at Sippar, Marduk at Babylon, Nabu at Borsippa. Such important deities were also represented at temples in other cities but the original site remained their 'home' on earth. The temple of the local god or goddess was seen as the vital centre of a city, its mark of identity and the very source of divine energy which protected and sustained all life within its boundaries. The destruction or desecration of sanctuaries was such an effective military strategy because without the presence of the local deity the city was vulnerable to all kinds of evil.

Although religious traditions in Mesopotamia were moulded by a literate temple hierarchy which preserved long-established ritual practices, new ideas and concepts emerged at times while others fell into obsolescence. The pantheon and cultic repertoire of the Babylonians, already in the Old Babylonian period, differs in many ways from that of the time of the Third Dynasty of Ur. First of all, the king's connection to the great gods of the land was reinterpreted in such a way as to stress his stewardship of the land rather than his divinity. The ancient Sumerian rite of the Sacred Marriage which symbolised the king's incorporation into the divine was abandoned never to be revived again. The famous scene in the *Epic of Gilgamesh* where the hero emphatically and rudely spurns Ishtar's offer of marriage and eternal life epitomised the Babylonian rejection of this idea. There was also a gradual phasing-out of many of the old female deities; some previously distinct goddesses merged, representing a particular aspect such as mother-goddesses,[8] healing goddesses (Gula taking over from Ninisisia and others), or they were 'married off' to assume the role of a spouse to a male deity (a process that had started already in the late third millennium: Ninlil became the wife of Enlil, Ningal that of the moon god Nanna-Suen, Aya of the sun god Shamash, and so forth). Sometimes a myth explained how these nuptials came to pass; a good Babylonian example is the account of how Ereshkigal, the Lady of the Underworld, lost her independence to Nergal because she could no longer bear her loneliness and fell for the charms of the celestial god Nergal once she had secured his visit to her shadowy domain.[9] Even Ishtar, the battle-loving seductress and embodiment of libidinous love, was officially tied to the great sky god Anu, at least according to a hymn from the Kassite period.[10] In other cases a new male god simply replaced a previously female deity, so for instance when Nabu, son of Marduk, took over the function of patron god of scribes from the Sumerian goddess Nisaba.

A genre of cult literature was devoted to the amorous relations between divine couples, most famous are those of Nabu and Tashmetum and the enigmatic love triangle scenario involving Marduk, his wife Sarpanitum and his 'silvery girl' Ishtar.[11] It was also a feature of the larger Babylonian temples to have marital quarters that feature a 'bed of delight', not unlike those still found in some south Indian temples today.[12] However, in comparison to the texts that had been written in Sumerian and which were still current in the Old Babylonian times, there is less emphasis on sexual imagery.[13]

Another important development was the tendency towards a 'personal god' which can first be observed in the Old Babylonian period (see below). The idea that each person has a supernatural, benevolent and protective guardian spirit may have older origins, and goes back to the notion of a mediator conveying prayers to the more elevated celestial gods. It was to play a significant part in the later apotropaic and healing rituals. Ultimately, the most characteristic development of Babylonian religion was the extraordinary fusion of religion and magic into a coherent although protean body of thought and practice which aimed at once to interpret the fundamental design of divine intention and procure protection and deliverance from sin and suffering. The great gods, most notably Marduk (as well as his father Ea and son Asarluhhi/Nabu), were invoked as master-magicians who know the appropriate incantations and who engage in a constant cosmic struggle against the myriad manifestations of evil. While the daily care of the gods, their provision with sacrifice and offerings, continued in a time-honoured way, the greatest creative effort was directed towards ever more efficacious ways of predicting the will of the gods and at the same time averting their nefarious effects on human beings.

In the first millennium, when after centuries of economic and political disasters the country experienced an extraordinary reversal of fortunes as a hugely wealthy empire, the gods of Babylonia were to be rewarded by lavish gifts and brand-new temples. The Neo-Babylonian kings, from Nebuchadnezzar II to Nabonidus, all dedicated themselves to religious building projects on an unprecedented scale while at the same time temple offices became ever more diverse with the elaboration of services and rituals. Even when political independence was lost after the Achaemenid conquest, Babylonian temples continued to flourish, not only economically but as centres of learning and research.

Nothing is known about the spiritual dimension of Late Babylonian religion at an age when all kinds of creeds were represented in a city such as Babylon with its Greek, Jewish, Persian and other communities, where all kinds of prophets and holy men declared the superiority of their own gods. In the end, the Babylonian gods, tied as they were to their cities and their ancient mud-brick temples, were forsaken in the deserted ruins while fragments of thoughts and gestures, knowledge and practice, survived, unrecognisable, as scattered remains within many later religious systems of the Near East and beyond.

TEMPLE ARCHITECTURE

The most tangible manifestations of Babylonian religious life are the remains of temples (Fig. 4.1). Archaeologists identify a building as a temple on the following grounds: by its size, the internal distribution of rooms — especially the presence of an oblong 'cella' with a niche — and the presence of architectural elaborations, such as evenly spaced recesses in some of the main walls. Fortunately the Babylonians had a habit of depositing foundation documents within the foundations or walls of a temple which would specify the name of the deity, the temple, and the king who had undertaken the restoration of the structure. While the archaeological investigations can detect the placement of walls, their relative thickness and articulation and work out the circulation patterns (given that the walls are preserved to a sufficient height or that lintels and door sockets remained in place), they can not reconstruct elevations. The

Figure 4.1 Reconstructed Babylonian temple of the goddess Nisaba at Tell Harmal (ancient Shaduppum). It dates from the beginning of the second millennium and shows the recessed façade typical for Mesopotamian sanctuaries, as well as two lions guarding the entrance. (Photo H.D. Galter)

question as to the original height of walls or whether some spaces were open to the sky or covered, cannot be answered with any certainty.[14] On occasion the debris recovered on the site gives an indication of the use or function of a space, but more often every valuable item had been moved or plundered. Some Babylonian texts referring to activities in the temple or ritual instructions help to gain a better understanding of how a temple worked as an architectural ensemble although the terminology used for parts of the building is notoriously ambiguous. There was not even a special word for 'temple'; it was simply called 'house of a God'.

Of great importance for the structural stability and the spiritual integrity of a temple were the foundations. They were thought to provide a link with the lower strata of the universe, to reach down to the Apsu and thus anchor the temple to the chthonian depths. Since any change in the plan of a temple was potentially dangerous as upsetting the cosmic balance, the Babylonians preferred to keep on repairing the walls on the razed stumps of the older ones rather

than dig into the foundations. The result was not only a long continuity of an existing layout but a gradual raising of the floor level
when the older remains were sealed under a new platform while
the walls were built above the previous ones. In the relatively rare
case of rebuilding a temple on a different site, it was a matter of
highest importance to determine the right date for the works
to begin – ascertained through omens – and that the building site
be properly purified. Nebuchadnezzar II's account of the rebuilding
of Marduk's temple at Babylon is a good example. Furthermore,
since the foundations represented the blueprint of the whole structure, all the walls were laid out below ground. Drainage channels
composed of baked brick segments were also incorporated at that
stage. Then came a level platform to seal the lower levels and the
actual temple rose above, 'raising its head high' according to the
old temple hymns, which endow the whole building with the
vitality of a living being.

Babylonian temples were thus visible from afar and towered
above the city quarters. However, unlike the Greek temples on
their acropolis with their columned porticoes and the doors of the
sanctuary open to the public gaze, Babylonian temples were enclosed
behind perimeter walls and only a certain class of priests were ever
admitted to their inner rooms. But since temples were not only
sanctuaries that contained the divine image but complex households where a whole variety of tasks were performed, there were a
whole series of rooms, grouped around an open courtyard, which
could accommodate these household tasks. The service of the gods
demanded regular offerings but the Babylonian gods, unlike their
Syrian or Roman counterparts, were not just presented with blood
sacrifices or 'holocausts' (burnt sacrifices) but with exquisitely
cooked food prepared in the temple kitchens,[15] and poured liquid
offerings (libations), such as beer, oil and wine. Smoke offerings
were also important and various resins were burnt to produce the
fragrance to delight the deities and mask unpleasant smells of
slaughter.

The layout of a Babylonian temple now becomes more clear; there
is usually one entrance to the whole precinct, a tunnel-like passage
which penetrates the thick perimeter walls. Two or more transverse
narrow guard-chambers follow before a larger, square or rectangular
space is reached which gives access to rooms distributed around its

sides. In this courtyard, called *kisalmahum*,[16] votive offerings were displayed, such as stelae or statues dedicated by kings and high officials.[17] From there a further space, usually open to the sky, would equally be surrounded by rooms on all sides, one of which would be distinguished by a façade decorated with niches and shallow, narrow buttresses. This harboured the gods' quarters. A centrally placed doorway, again set into the thick brickwork, leads either directly, or through an ante-chamber, into the sanctuary, a large, oblong chamber,[18] which was designated as *kissum* or *kummum*.[19] The statue of the deity would be placed on a pedestal (Babylonian *parakkum*) within a niche which could either be placed along the short wall or opposite the entrance, along the long side of the chamber. A low altar-like platform stood in front of the pedestal to receive the offerings. There were usually subsidiary chambers which could also be reached from the main cult room ('cella'), serving as private rooms for the gods, sometimes called *bit eršim*, 'bed-room'. At least some temples had accessible roofs which were used for particular rituals.

Such were the amenities of most medium-sized temples. There were of course also much smaller chapel-like sanctuaries in every city. In very important religious sites the temple precinct could also incorporate a ziggurat, or 'temple-tower'. This was an entirely separate structure, usually not physically connected to the temple of the ground (the 'low temple') as was the custom in Assyria but free-standing, sometimes surrounded by its own perimeter wall. A ziggurat was entirely solid, built of a core of mudbrick which could be faced with a mantle of burnt brick, in superimposed stages which diminished in size towards the top. Only the highest level was used for ritual purposes, an elevated platform where the 'high temple' (Old Babylonian *gegunnum*; Neo-Babylonian *nuhar*) was placed. Access to the top was by means of ramps, both lateral and perpendicular to the facing of the ziggurat. No ziggurats have survived enough to reconstruct either access or the high temple with any certainty. Ziggurats monumentalised one of the aspects of every temple, to serve as a link between heaven and earth. They were also described as sacred mountains, thought to be attractive to the gods because of their height and their distance from the noisy proximity of humanity.

TEMPLE PERSONNEL

Babylonian temples, especially in important cities, needed a large staff to administer the agricultural production and distribution, to fulfil a variety of domestic services, as well as to maintain the cultic duties towards the gods. It is interesting to note that there was not a general division between secular and religious offices, between a 'priesthood' solely devoted to the service of the gods, and any other personnel. In fact there is no word in Akkadian that corresponds to the notion of 'priest' such as it was used in the Bible, to denote those among the servants of the temple who had access to the inner sanctum. We have the titles of hundreds of temple officials and we can see from the temple archives that there was a hierarchical structure with some officials having higher status and receiving larger renumerations than others. According to some temple archives there appears to be a distinction between 'full-time' and 'part-time' staff. Charpin in his study of the temples at Ur during the time of Hammurabi has shown that some offices were alienable, and divisible in time – like a timeshare. They could be bought and sold and divided up upon inheritance. The 'full-time' positions on the other hand always maintained their integrity and passed undivided from father to one son only.[20] It has become customary to call the former positions 'prebends', the latter – *faute de mieux* – 'priests'. But such categorisation remains misleading since the duties carried out by prebendaries could be seen to have cultic relevance, such as that of the 'sweepers' who were not simply cleaners but had purificatory roles as well. Many such offices, however, were not closely tied to any particular function and most of them were simply designated by the name of the deity they served, sometimes for just a few days a year.[21] It stands to reason that the services these people rendered were of a nature that lent itself easily to a timeshare principle, those of an honorific nature or those that could be carried out without particular expertise. They could look after part of the cult equipment or votive offerings, for instance, or be concerned with general purificatory services, such as the above mentioned 'sweepers', the 'door-keepers', and similarly vague appellations which are not clearly understood. We have seen that even a small share in such a prebend was worth holding on to economically, and in addition it must have had a certain prestige because prebendaries were generally from established and moneyed families.

A *nouveau-riche* would invest in a fair number of prebends to document his status and to enrich his social network.[22]

The full-time temple staff looked after all the other services needed to guarantee the smooth running of the institution in all its different aspects, be they administrative or cultic. They comprised managers, executives, archivists, accountants, secretaries and the whole range of functionaries in charge of different sectors of the economic side of the temple; as well as those who dealt with the ritual sector, purifiers, chanters, musicians and singers, diviners, exorcists, recitors of particular types of chants and prayers; those who looked after the divine images in a cult context and those who repaired them – a whole range of services for which there is no common denominator in Akkadian but a bewildering number of titles which may have quite different connotations over time and which varied from temple to temple.

In the Late Babylonian period the terminology for temple personnel changed.[23] Persons who had access to the sacred precincts of the temple were called *erib biti*, literally 'enterer of the temple'. They included persons who performed a variety of rituals and included diviners, exorcists, and those craftsmen who came in touch with cult furnishings, but excluded brewers and bakers.[24] The function of *erib biti* was a prebendary office and as such not a professional (full-time) temple position, unlike that of the *šangu* or *šešgallu* (literally 'big brother', it denotes the chief priest). However, there were differences in just how surplus income from the temple was distributed; in some temples all personnel received rations, in others only the manual workers, while more senior officials received prebends or salaries. At Uruk, for instance, during the Hellenistic period, the main source of income from a prebend constituted shares in the offerings presented to the gods at ritual meals – which did not just consist of the food but also the dishes used, wine, spices, cloths and so on[25] – while those persons who served in an official, performative (and presumably full-time) capacity were allotted a fixed salary.[26]

TEMPLE SERVICES

The central concern of a temple was of course the care for the divine images who resided there. Very few identifiable statues of

Babylonian gods or goddesses have survived, no doubt since many were made of precious materials which made them attractive to plunderers and looters. According to ancient descriptions the statues were clothed in sumptuous robes and adorned with crowns and jewels, all of which were periodically changed, rather like some Marian statues in Catholic pilgrimage churches to this day. The making of a cult image was accompanied by a whole range of purification rituals. Artisans had to be in a fit state to take on such an endeavour. When the carving, painting and smelting were over the statue had to be prepared to become charged with a divine life force. One text describes the lengthy ritual – called the Opening of the Mouth – which was meant to effect the transformation from a lifeless object into a deity.[27] After lengthy purification of the image its eyes, ears and mouth were touched with a special implement, while incantations were recited, to 'open' its organs of perception. Thereafter the god was taken to his quarters in the temple where he or she resided in the main cella during the day and was removed to a special chamber or niche for the night. Furthermore, a deity did not dwell in isolation at the temple but had an entourage of family and minor deities who were accommodated in separate cult-niches and included in the daily offerings. According to an Old Babylonian text which refers to a week-long festival at Larsa,[28] the ritual day began at the time of the evening breeze. In the morning the statue of the main deity and his or her divine family and entourage were prepared for the day and taken in procession to the main sanctuary. Priests followed in order of rank, accompanied by musicians and singers. Once in the main cella, grain offerings were presented and in the course of the day there followed at least three more ritual meals. At nightfall, the procedure was reversed and the images were returned to their niches while the main sanctuary door was closed. While temples were generally locked at night, there were occasions for night-time vigils and even torch-lit processions. All the activities were performed according to a strict liturgy with appropriate hymns and prayers, the accompaniment of music, to praise and laud and to remind the deities to extend their benevolence towards their subjects and their city. The rhythms of the year, such as the phases of the moon, the appearance and disappearance of planets and stars, determined the liturgical calendar. They were particularly important for the

astral deities, such as the moon god Sin, and Ishtar who was associated with the planet Venus, but it seems that most temples
observed the lunar cycles with special rituals which emphasised the
cosmic nature of the deities.[29]

A very important aspect which permeates all relations towards
the divine in Babylonian religion is the notion of purity. We see
in the temple archives that a variety of persons performed purificatory functions, which embrace both what we consider hygienic –
the absence of physical dirt and contamination – and the ritual
purity, defined as the absence of evil spirits.[30] In order to maintain
or to re-establish this purity, which was a prerequisite for any
contact with the divine, persons and objects had to be cleansed and
washed physically, as well as ritually through the recitation of
special incantations and the burning of aromatics and incense.[31] It
has to be imagined that much of the daily activities around the
Babylonian sanctuaries were dedicated to this task. As in all sectors
of personnel, purification specialists were ranked, with the top
position being held by the *sanga-mah*, who may have had a particular connection with the presentation of food to the deities and the
priests' hand-washing;[32] the title is usually translated as 'chief
chanter'.

PRIESTLY INITIATION

In order for a person to be admitted to the presence of the divine
he had to undergo an initiation which rendered him pure. He also
had to be examined physically to determine whether he was free
from bodily defects and in the right frame of mind. A much copied
text, probably going back to the end of the second millennium,
describes the rituals that were carried out for an unspecified priestly
office at the Enlil temple at Nippur.[33] The neophyte was received
by a *nišakku* priest of Enlil or Ninlil, a *šešgallu* and a 'barber'. They
led him into the ablutions room and inspected his body from head
to toes; only somebody with a body 'as clean as a statue made of
gold' and 'filled with reverence and humility' was allowed to enter
the temple of Enlil. He must also never have shed blood, have
defective eyesight or have been 'beaten with stocks or whips' as a
punishment for theft or robbery. Then he was washed by the barber

while the other priests recited incantions at all stages – over the water that poured over his head, over the soap, the razor used to shave his head, and the cloth that dried his body. The incantations were meant to ward off evil and to cleanse the candidate.

The recitation or chanting of liturgies was an integral part of Babylonian temple services and performed by specialists who trained in particular categories and there are a whole range of titles to designate them; the *kalu*, for instance, sang lamentations to soothe the angry hearts of the gods; they had to select appropriate and sometimes very lengthy chants from a vast repertoire to suit particular occasions. The *galaturru* and *galamahhu* (perhaps the titles denote distinctions in rank rather than expertise) also chanted and performed, especially on special occasions and festivals, while the *naru* ('singer') was responsible for the entertainment of the deities on a daily basis.

Of special interest are the so-called cultic actors, known as *assinnu* and *kurgarru*. They had particular connections with the temple of Ishtar and wore special clothing,[34] which seems to signal a transgender identity.[35] It has been suggested that in the early period (perhaps up to the Old Babylonian period) they may have performed ecstatic rituals in a trance state because of their connections with the underworld (mentioned in some myths) and their special instrument, the frame drum, a favourite instrument of ecstatics in many cultures. In the second millennium they sang or recited their liturgies in a special form of Sumerian, known as *eme.sal* – used in the texts by female deities. In the first millennium they appear regularly in processions and festivals associated with Ishtar but they also had an important role to play in apotropaic and curative rituals.

PRIVATE DEVOTIONS AND PERSONAL GODS

The most obvious way for Babylonians to express their piety and devotion to particular gods was to give their children theophoric names.[36] Most personal names were in fact short sentences denoting particular sentiments or wishes: 'Marduk is the father of the weak' (Abi-enshi-Marduk), 'I have asked of Adad' (Adad-erish), 'I trust in my lady' (Ana-beltiia-taklatu) , 'May he reach old age, o Shamash'

(Liltambir-Shamash), and so on. Women usually bore names referring to goddesses. The study of people's personal names can reveal much of the relative popularity of deities in a place and period.

Temple liturgies were primarily directed towards the 'care and feeding of the gods'.[37] To what extent temples catered for the spiritual needs of human beings is much more difficult to determine. Individuals could make donations – from humble offerings to slaves and valuable cult furniture – which constituted gifts to the deities, to 'make their hearts glow'. The protagonist of the Babylonian poem *ludlul bel nemeqi* ('I will praise the Lord of Wisdom'), who like the Biblical Job is inflicted with a variety of physical and mental suffering, turns to the temple of Marduk, the Esagila 'with prostration and supplication' and performs various devotions at the different gates of the temple:

> In the 'Gate of Release from Guilt' I was released from
> my bond,
> In the 'Gate of Worship' my mouth inquired,
> In the 'Gate of Resolving of Sighs' my sighs were
> resolved,
> In the 'gate of Pure Water' I was sprinkled with water
> of purification,
> In the 'Gate of Well-Being' I communed with Marduk,
> In the 'Gate of Exuberance' I kissed the foot of Sarpanitum.
> I persisted in supplication and prayer before them.
> Fragrant incense I placed before them,
> I presented an offering, a gift, accumulated donations,
> I slaughtered fat oxen, and butchered fattened sheep,
> I repeatedly libated honey-sweet beer and pure wine.[38]

This passage seems to suggest that there were amenities outside the inner sanctuary where people could appeal personally to divine intermediaries. In general a Babylonian temple was not a place for communal or private worship. Of course the prebend system allowed at least some members of the public to participate to a greater or smaller extent in liturgical ceremonies at the temple but ordinary citizens did not need to get involved since their devotions seem to have been primarily addressed to their 'personal gods' (*ilum* but also referred to as *lamassu* or *šedu*) in a private setting. In Old Babylonian

Ur houses Leonard Woolley discovered niches and similar arrangements which he identified as private altars, as well as figurines which possibly represented deities.[39]

Literary prayers from this period also stress the attachment to 'one's (own) god' (*ilum*). The personal god was not one of the great gods of the Babylonian pantheon, not even the god invoked in one's personal name, but a protective supernatural guiding spirit who like a guardian angel (the customary translation of *lamassu*) guided his protégé through life, protected him (or her) from harm and interceded for him with the celestial deities. Since one's 'own god' was thought to be intimately associated with the person, any illness or misfortune he experienced as the result of malevolent influences or of 'sin' also affected his god.[40] In order to re-establish the vitality of both god and human being, a ritual known as 'Mouth Washing' could be performed.[41] This consisted of two parts: first, the revitalisation of the personal god who was reborn through the symbolic enactment of a birth-process; and thereafter that of the human subject who was placed in a sort of magical cage indicated by lines drawn with flour and washed with various substances. A portable stove was also used into which the officiant threw seven images. Incantations are spoken throughout, and the afflicted had to be 'judged' before he was free to leave the cage, cleansed with incense, and waved over with a flaming torch. In this manner the proper relationship between the person and the god was re-established. What is not made explicit in this text, and indeed in many similar ritual instructions, is where this ritual was to take place, whether it had to be performed in a temple or a private house for instance. However, it is clear that the men who performed such services formed part of the temple institution.

COMBATING EVIL; EXORCISM AND HEALING RITUALS

Like many peoples in traditional societies the Babylonians ascribed persistent ill fortune and chronic disease to supernatural forces. It was possible to see these as random and unaccountable attacks by innately malevolent beings, such as demons and evil spirits, also snakes, scorpions and even dogs.[42] Sumerian incantations and rituals focused on combating these demonic beings and on freeing victims from their baleful influences by symbolically transferring the negative attribute to a neutral carrier which could be destroyed. This relatively simple view of the nature of evil was supplemented with other aetiologies, such as the idea that the gods, in their fundamental unpredictability or in their wisdom which human beings can never comprehend, could directly and also adversely affect someone's health and well-being. This was known as the 'Hand of the God/des' and there were specific rituals and incantations to 'calm the heart' of the angry deity.[43] A different view, propagated by the priesthood since the Old Babylonian period, introduced the notion that suffering was a deserved punishment for sin and sent by the gods as 'harmful divine intervention'.[44] This made it necessary to define sin not only as a transgression against ethical codes and as such the result of deliberate human behaviour but as a state of being brought about through contact with ritually polluting substances. The cure was to re-establish untroubled relations between the gods and the 'sinner' through purification to replace the negative force with a positive one, or as expressed in an incantation: 'May the evil *udug* and the evil *galla* stand aside, May the good *udug* and the good *galla* be present.' Another baneful influence were human beings who as witches and sorcerers harmed those of their family members and neighbours who had made them envious, jealous and resentful. These negative emotions were able to materialise into an evil force which would attack the victim. Such diverse beliefs about the sources of illness and bad luck reflect different views of man's place in the world and to what extent he sees himself threatened by powerful forces beyond his control. Witchcraft beliefs and the fear of venomous animals are reactions to immediate dangers – of psychological and emotional states or the effects of poison and infection. In traditional societies the cure of the former generally involves a thorough investigation of a range of potentially troubled social relationships.[45] In the urban society of Mesopotamia it was one of the other major functions of the temple institution to channel the anxieties of the populace regarding their exposure to evil influences from unknown sources into a more coherent framework. Not only were the demons being counted and named, and their relationship to the great gods defined as ultimately inferior, all counteracting treatment and palliatives were institutionalised so that as far as Babylonia (or indeed any other Mesopotamian culture) was concerned there was no distinction between 'magic' and 'religion'. Indeed it was one of the main reasons for the tenacity of Mesopotamian civilisation that the supernatural causes of human suffering were investigated and confronted in a comprehensive manner.

Some of the often invoked agents of ill-fortune are the restless spirits of unburied corpses. Also the spirits of dead relatives could threaten the well-being of the living. Therefore a body had to be buried with due respect, often within the precincts of the family house, and libations of pure water were regularly offered to assuage the perpetual thirst of the dead in the underworld. An often expressed Babylonian prejudice against the nomadic populations was that 'they did not bury their dead'. Living at close quarters with other family members or neighbours can be a source of conflict in all societies. In periods of instability and with increased competition for daily survival, psychological tensions can lead to accusations of witchcraft. In Mesopotamia women and especially foreign women, such as those who entered a household as captured slaves, were often regarded as potential witches, and it was their spittle and their 'evil tongue' which could serve as an instrument to harness evil against those they hated or envied.[46] In Babylonia, even in the periods of great social change, such as in the eighteenth century BC, the authorities made great efforts to stem potential outbreaks of witchcraft accusations. In the Code of Hammurabi, the second promulgation, just after homicide, specified that unsubstantiated witchcraft accusations should incur capital punishment.[47] Since mere repression would hardly have been effective, the perceived danger from human agents of evil was met by professional exorcists, trained and maintained by the temples. Destructive human agents of evil became conceptually integrated in the whole host of antagonistic supernatural forces. They could all be banned and neutralised by invoking the superior powers of the great gods, especially the divine master-magicians such as Ea, Asarluhhi and Marduk, in highly formalised and specifically targeted rituals. Older traditions of exorcism which had been transmitted in Sumerian formed the basis for increasing elaboration in scope and precision so that it took years to perfect the arts of the *ašipu*. Tzvi Abusch has demonstrated how the figure of the witch, from its origin in

117

the folk tradition of a frustrated woman, became invested with ever greater supernatural stature as the powers and expertise of her opponent grew.[48] This is well reflected in the grand anti-sorcery series known as 'Burning' (*maqlu*) which grew from ten incantations to one hundred and finally envisages the witch no longer as a dangerous human being who had to be killed but 'as a cosmic force that must be thrown off its course and placed in limbo so that it may not be able to continue moving on its path between this world and the netherworld'.[49] In the first millennium anti-sorcery texts we also find the notion that all perpetrators of evil, be they of human or superhuman origin, witches and demons alike, are regarded as criminals to be judged and punished, to death or banishment, by the gods. The performance of *maqlu* had always included the destruction by fire of an effigy of the witch. In its final versions from the seventh century, the ritual had become a dramatic performance, the result of generations of scholarly reflection and expertise. While only the elite and the royal family could avail themselves of such a costly and lengthy ceremony,[50] less elaborate forms of exorcism would suffice for the less well-off population. On the whole it appears that exorcists generally had a lower rank within the hierarchy than diviners and chief administrators which seems to relate to a sliding scale of their knowledge and skill.[51]

People could also protect themselves from all kinds of harm by apotropaic amulets, statues and spells.[52] But to render such devices efficacious they had to be magically charged through rituals. One text, for instance, describes how a new house could be suitably purified and magically protected to 'block the progress of evil' and so that 'sorcery will not approach the house of the man'.[53]

> [When some]one's gate is purified, sulphur, gypsum, and
> red paste together you shall crush,
> you mix it [into *billatu*-liquid] and Incantation 'You are
> fierce you are violent' [thrice] you shall recite [over it], the
> door-post of the gates of the house of the man with the
> sediment
> [you shall smear?] after the *billatu*-liquid into which you
> have mixed (the ingredients)
> [you shall ...] and wash over the sediment'.
> Sorcery will not approach the house of the man.[54]

In all such prophylactic and curative rituals, the recitation of powerful incantations was of the utmost importance. Some of the words were so well known to the practitioners that the texts only indicate the incipient words. There was obviously a matter of routine involved, although the Babylonian exorcists displayed great creativity in inventing ever new and more powerful formulae to invoke the assistance of the great gods of magic and how to counteract evil influence. However, only with the accompanying actions did the incantation become effective because they materially bound the uttered word to the performative dynamic of the ritual. The materials and substances used were chosen because of their perceived magical properties which may have been based on a linguistic relationship such as a pun, or on cosmic affinities between certain colours, metals, numbers, and the gods. The actions manipulate these substances and symbols in a way which expresses their purpose; washing and fumigating disperse and cleanse and dissolve, burning destroys, the tying and untying of knots fixes or undoes the incantation, and so on. The timing too was appropriate to the powers evoked. *Maqlu* for instance begins at night since the deities of the night were called up; those which appealed to Shamash, the sun god, were held at sunrise or midday.

The huge number of apotropaic and exorcist rituals developed during the second and first millennia covered any eventuality and affliction. It proves that the temple institutions took the responsibility for the psychological and physical well-being of the citizens very seriously indeed. As with many curative systems, however, the more cures and spells the greater the choice and the difficulty in finding the right one. The written versions of incantations and the accompanying rituals formed an essential compendium to assist the professional exorcist but only very few libraries could boast a complete range of all available sources. The Assyrian kings ordered the Babylonian temple collections to be raided for their precious and potent tablets. In fact many of the most complex rituals were adapted or even invented to suit the needs of powerful monarchs some of whom, like Esarhaddon, felt themselves particularly vulnerable to supernatural attacks. On the whole, the services of the legitimate 'white magician' were meant to reassure king and slave alike that all manner of evil which could threaten mankind could ultimately be controlled within the universal framework in which gods and men were tied by mutual obligation. While the sheer number of exorcistic and curative rituals may point to a high degree of anxiety in Babylonian society, it also demonstrates the effort made by the temple institutions to alleviate and control suffering.

DIVINATION

Divinatory practices are well attested in Mesopotamia since the third millennium. Divination works on the principle that there are causal connections between events and actions which are pre-established. On a sliding time continuum the past was seen as tied to the future in an internally coherent way informed by divine intelligence. In Mesopotamia this was expressed by the notion that the gods decide 'the fate' (Babylonian *šimtu*) of the world. In various mythological accounts, such as the Creation Epic *enuma elish*, this is described like a meeting of a council. Having deliberated in their hearts on the 'design' of things to come, the gods pronounce their 'decision' (*purussu*) as the manifestation of their will which is then inscribed on the Tablets of Destiny. This divine document contained the destinies of every living thing in the universe, the movement of the stars and planets, and the innermost characteristics of all components of creation. While the grand design of creation can never be comprehended by mankind, the gods were seen to allow channels of communication to reveal their decisions to their human subjects who were after all created to fulfil obligations towards their divine lords. In the myths the gods speak directly to their servants – as Ea does when he warns Atrahasis of the impending flood. However, such direct means of transmitting divine messages were not common in Babylonia. Possession cults, for instance, where gods communicate through the mouth of a person in trance, were not unknown but did not become part of an institutional setting.[55] Dreams were another avenue of receiving divine guidance. Gudea, a ruler of the Sumerian city of Lagash in the late third millennium, described on a stone statue how he had spent the night in the temple of his city god and how the plan and dimension of a new temple was revealed to him in a dream. Again, this case remained exceptional and the practice of soliciting such direct divine revelations was not encouraged by the Babylonian priesthood. On the other hand, dreams could not be ruled out completely as a medium for transmitting supernatural communications. They formed part of a wide range of observable phenomena, on earth and in the heavens, which could signify portents of divine 'designs' and be read as ominous.[56] The collection and the interpretation of such omina became one of the most highly developed branches of Babylonian intellectual endeavours.[57] The most comprehensive series of omen compendia which dealt with terrestrial matters, known as *šumma alu* ('if a city'),[58] comprised more than 120 tablets. As indicated by the title taken from the initial line, this begins with the way cities were built, and goes on to architecture, the behaviour of animals, the growth of trees and plants, as well as human activities, from hygienic to sexual practices. Its celestial counterpart, known as *Enuma Anu Enlil* was based on observations of the planets and stars.[59] Another series (*šumma izbu*) was dedicated to teratological phenomena, mainly malformations in human or animal foetuses.[60] A large number of divinatory texts were concerned with the interpretation of solicited omen responses, which I will discuss presently.

The format of all these works was structurally similar. An omen consists of two parts: a protasis and an apodosis. The protasis, expressed as a hypothetical occurrence, describes the phenomenon: for example, 'If the sun is surrounded by a halo and a cloud bank lies on the right', or 'If a man has intercourse with a woman but has a premature ejaculation so that he squirted sperm over himself', or 'If a new-born child has no left ear'. An apodosis or explanation immediately follows the protasis. This was always phrased as an inevitable, about-to-happen event with regards to the well-being or destruction of an individual, the king, or the country which reflects the original divinatory enquiries (for example, 'there will be catastrophe in the country', 'the god will hear his prayer', 'the enemy will invade the land'). The interpretations are partly based on general conventions of divination, left is negative, right is positive, light is positive, dark is negative, two negative signs make one positive and so on, but one can also see them as primarily scholastic elaborations of a conceptual pattern which can also be detected in the Babylonian lexicographic tradition.[61] It is concerned with detecting principles of order and causality in the apparent jumble of disparate phenomena, using a variety of guidelines which may have phonetic, epigraphic, literary or historical connotations. There is also a tendency for the genre to develop its own momentum since it invites all logical possibilities to be pursued, regardless of their seeming absurdity (such as deformed ears growing out of buttocks or astronomically impossible planetary configurations). In their adherence to an internal logic omen interpretations could be compared to the 'absurd' solutions of Lewis Carroll's syllogisms[62] or even Wittgensteinian 'language games'.[63] They also show very clearly how the Babylonian scholars built an enormous edifice of data in an attempt to emulate the hidden grand design that inspired creation. Since the basic tenet of Babylonian metaphysics ruled out randomness and coincidence within an intelligently created universe – both these notions are a by product of 'modernity'[64] – their task was as deeply meaningful to adepts as the numeric-mystical calculations of the Kabbalists were to Jewish scholars. It is also important to realise, as Veldhuis has pointed out, that the omen collections did not have a practical purpose, such as to provide a reference work for practising diviners.[65] The product of many centuries of compilation and structuring, by the time of the seventh century they comprised many thousands of entries, and existed *sui generis* as a repository of esoteric knowledge.

DIVINATION RITUALS

While the above mentioned omen compendia loom large in the consciousness of contemporary Assyriologists who have by default inherited the literary bequest of Babylonian scholars, they had much less impact on those people in ancient Babylonia who sought guidance and reassurance in their daily affairs. Their needs were met, in so far as they had the necessary funds, by the diviners (*baru*) employed by the temple institutions. The procedure common to all oracular decisions was for the enquirer to formulate a specific set of questions and the oracle (or rather the gods who control the oracle) to be invited to respond in a straightforward yes or no answer.[66] It constitutes a direct appeal to deities asking them to reveal their intent. Such practices seem to have a long history in Mesopotamia and were at first used to determine which candidate among a number of suitable pretenders was to be chosen for high offices within the temple institution.[67] However, we ignore the exact mechanism of the oracle since such matters were not committed to writing before the Old Babylonian period. From then on there were a variety of sources, training tablets and model organs, references in administrative texts and royal inscriptions, and, especially from the first millennium, reports by diviners to the royal court. The most popular form of Mesopotamian oracle was the examination of the internal organs of sacrificial animals, mainly sheep. The person who sought an oracular response would furnish the required animal, which had to be free from blemish and preferably unshorn. The *baru* then addressed one or more of the gods (often Marduk and Shamash) to write their answer to the stated question on the entrails of the sheep to be sacrificed. After the slaughter he investigated the internal organs, proceeding from the top (the windpipe) to the bottom (the coils of the intestines to the colon). He looked for any abnormalities in the appearance of the exta, paying particular attention to the surface of the lungs and the liver which was divided into different sectors and zones (Fig. 4.2). The placing (right, left, top, bottom and so on) of any distinguishing marks here was highly relevant, as was the direction of the mark which was referred to as *kakku* ('the weapon'): pointing to the left was negative, pointing to the right positive. He then gave the report, either orally when the examination of the inner organs had been performed in the presence of the client, or in writing, which summarised the question and the indications as either favourable or unfavourable, having added up all the positive and negative marks.

Other, less elaborate, oracular practices were the smoke oracle, where the diviner squatted above a flat vessel on which aromatics and resin were burned, the oil oracle for which oil was poured on the surface of a liquid such as wine, and the interpretation of the flight of birds.

It took a long time to train for the profession of a *baru* because of the highly technical and specialised knowledge involved. Especially the arts of extispicy, where the lungs, liver and colon of a freshly slaughtered sheep were examined, became very complex in the Old Babylonian period. The practitioners had to be free from bodily defects; they were under special obligation to maintain a high degree of ritual purity and of course they needed to be literate. In practice the office usually passed from father to son. The status

Figure 4.2 Old Babylonian clay model of a sheep's liver, c. 1700 BC. It shows how the organ was divided into distinct areas and the text refers to the ominous implications of any mark in that place. (© British Museum)

of a fully trained and skilled diviner was very high, and although most diviners operated within temple organisations, they could also be employed by the palace; one such *baru*, called Asqudum, played an important role at the court of Mari for instance;[68] others rose to great prominence in the service of Assyrian kings.[69] It was at the Assyrian court that interpreters of astronomical phenomena, who quite often were also trained in the arts of divination and the 'soothing of the angry heart of gods', came to perfect their specialisation in such a way as to be able to predict potentially dangerous celestial configurations such as eclipses.[70] In the late first millennium, when there was no longer an indigenous court in Babylonia, the most popular form of oracular practice was astrology in which the observation of planetary movements combined with the tradition of omen interpretation. By the time of the Seleucid period, the astrologer had replaced the *baru* as the most prestigious omen specialist.

Despite the great variety of means which had been invented to ascertain the hidden will of the gods, the knowledge thus obtained was not necessarily comforting or reassuring. Unfavourable pronouncements and negative omina were deeply upsetting. We hear that some kings asked for several repetitions of the oracle or invited 'second opinions' by rival practitioners. There was always the possibility that signs had been misread or that some fault in the performance invalidated the conclusion and it appears from the reports that the diviners could continue their search until the expected 'favourable' pronouncement was obtained. However, to forestall the disquieting effect of a negative verdict and of evil portents (revealed in a dream for instance), the Babylonian priests devised a possible solution. This was no less than an attempt to persuade the gods to revoke their decisions and 'change the unfavourable judgement to a favourable one'. Once you presume to communicate with the gods, as by inviting them to transcribe their will in a manner intelligible to man, and if they were generally willing to lend an ear to the entreaties and prayers of the human subjects, then they could likewise be expected to cede to persuasion. The threatening and destructive 'fate' did not inevitably have to come to pass; it could be averted by recourse to prayer, sacrifice and rituals. The ritual series known as *namburbi* contains instructions and incantations to redirect the course of 'fate'.[71] The aim of the ritual was to soothe the anger of the deity who had sent the omen. The theological justification for these rituals was the thought that 'the god who created the earthquake, Ea, had also created an apotropaic ritual against it'.[72] The afflicted person (primarily the king) had to undergo a lengthy purification to cleanse himself from the pollution that clings to the presence of a bad omen, as well as his house and environment. Then he needed to be reintegrated into normal living conditions and strengthened with a durable protection against any further threat of omina. Certain royal rituals, such as the practice of selecting a substitute king for particularly dangerous periods of time (such as an eclipse) who would attract the 'bad fate' to his person, shifted the target to secure the vitality of the ruler. That this was not meant to be a trick played to capricious deities is made clear by the admission of 'sin' by the real king, who is not only meant to become aware of his human frailty for committing sins against the gods, but is also told to 'be on his guard' and to adjust his behaviour.[73]

Omen decisions, whether solicited by sacrifice in order to determine a favourable date of an enterprise or to confirm a course of action, or whether received involuntarily through adverse circumstances and diagnosed as such retrospectively, alerted the Babylonians to the many dangers which beset all aspects of life.

The voluminous cuneiform literature on exorcisms and oracles gives the impression that survival was precarious and in a permanent state of lability. Were the Babylonians then prone to neurotic insecurity? There is an interesting text from the late second millennium which paints a picture of a person besieged by anxiety and suffering from what we would call acute depression:

My god has forsaken me and disappeared,
my goddess has failed me and keeps at a distance.
(....)
Fearful omens beset me.
I am got out of my house and wander outside.
The omen organs are confused and inflamed for me very
day.
The omen of the diviner and dream priest does not
explain my condition.
What is said in the street portends ill for me.
When I lie down at night, my dream is terrifying.
The king, the flesh of the gods, the sun of his peoples,
his heart is enraged (with me), and cannot be appeased.
The courtiers plot hostile action against me,
they assemble themselves and give utterance to impious
words.
Thus the first, 'I will make him pour out his life.'
The second says 'I will make him vacate his post.'
On this the third, 'I will seize his position.'
'I will taken over his estate', says the fourth.
(....)
Their hearts rage against me, and are ablaze like fire.

They combine against me in slander and lies.
(..)
I who strode along as a noble, have learned to slip by
unnoticed,
Though a dignitary, I have become a slave.
To my relations I am like a recluse.
If I walk the street, ears are pricked;
If I enter the palace, eyes blink.
My city frowns on me like an enemy;
Indeed my land is savage and hostile.
My friend has become my foe,
My companion has become a wretch and a devil.
(..)
When my acquantaince sees me, he passes by on the
other side.
My family treat me as an alien.
(...)
They have let another take my offices, and appointed an
outsider in my rites.
By day there is sighing, by night lamentation,
Monthly – wailing, each year – gloom.
I moan like a dove all my days;
[for a song] I emit groans.[74]

The text goes on to elaborate on the worsening condition of the
'patient' and that 'the diviner with his inspection did not get to
the root of the matter', nor did any libations or offering bring any
relief; on the contrary his condition worsens:

My lofty stature they destroyed like a wall
My robust figure they laid down like a bulrush,
I am thrown down like a bog plant and cast on my face.
The *alu*-demon has clothed himself in my body as a
garment;
Sleep covers me like a net.
My eyes stare but do not see,
My ears are open, but do not hear.
Feebleness has seized my whole body,
Concussion has fallen upon my flesh.

Paralysis has grasped my arms,
Impotence has fallen on my knees,[75]
My feet forgot their motion.
[A stroke] has got me, I choke like someone prostrate.
[..]...death, it has covered my face.[76]

He is only relieved from his suffering by a mysterious apparition in the guise of a 'remarkable young man of outstanding physique' and a 'young woman of shining countenance' who purify and heal the patient in a series of dreams. The text ends in a long prayer of gratitude to 'merciful Marduk whose heart was appeased'.

This composition paints a vivid picture of the reversals of fate which could beset a well-situated Babylonian official and plunge him into abject despair. Although he can avail himself of all expert help and does not shirk from costly sacrifices, he is unable to detect the cause of his suffering and it disappears as suddenly and as arbitrarily as it has come. Thus the wise man does well to remember that good fortune, health and happiness are randomly bestowed and randomly withheld by the gods. Themes of divine accountability – the problem of theodicy – are discussed in a similar composition in dialogue form. The 'just' sufferer takes a cynical view of the world in which evildoers succeed and good men are cast aside. Unlike in the Biblical account of Job which may have been inspired by this text, there is no epiphany by God to silence the complaints of Job, only a rather weak plea 'may the god who has thrown me off give help, may the goddess who has abandoned me show mercy'.[77] These literary compositions give some insight into the mentality of the educated Babylonian who is both cynically aware of the futility of religious precepts and yet persists in trusting to the old bonds which tied the gods to their creation.

5

MATERIAL CULTURE

HOUSING AND THE URBAN
ENVIRONMENT[1]

Babylonian cities were in appearance not unlike many Iraqi or west Syrian towns today where mud brick is still the main building material. Naturally they had no telegraph poles, asphalted roads, satellite dishes and no electricity to light up shops and houses at night. But archaeologists have been struck by the fact that many architectural features of simple residential building have persisted over the last four thousand years.[2]

In Babylonia, where the very soil was clay, there was no alternative to mud brick. Local trees, such as the date-palm, poplar and tamarisk, supplied roof timbers and materials for doors but could not have been used to build houses for the whole population. In the south of Iraq, the marsh dwellers construct their shelters and also very beautiful, large meeting houses from reeds. There are representations of reed buildings on early Mesopotamian artefacts and it is likely that such structures were much more common than the archaeological records suggest, since such constructions leave no visible trace.

In rural regions and the suburbs, the most common type of homestead consisted of a rectangular compound, surrounded by a pisé wall high enough to ensure privacy and entered by a single gateway. Along one or several sides were contiguous single-room units with one door each giving onto the courtyard which served a variety of purposes, such as preparing and cooking meals and other domestic tasks, as well as socialising. Dome-shaped clay ovens and fire-places were standard equipment, as were large clay storage vessels. The individual rooms served as storage, sleeping quarters and stables. The number of rooms was relative to the size of a family; a young couple would start with just two to three units and then gradually add more as the household expanded. Owing to the intense heat of the summer months and strong glare of the sun, window openings were kept to a minimum and were placed directly below the roof line in order to avoid weakening the mud brick walls. The flat roofs were made by laying trunks of poplars or boards of palm-trees directly onto the mud brick walls. The timbers were then covered with a thick coating of mud. Mud plaster was also liberally applied on the outside and inside of the walls to seal them from vermin and protect them from erosion and damage. The floors inside were made of hardened and polished earth. Domestic animals, such as dogs, goats and donkeys for transport, were kept in the compound at night. Most houses did not have a separate water supply – women had to go to the nearby canal to fill the clay containers in the homestead. Richer families could afford to expand and elaborate on this basic layout, especially by having upper storeys and a more complex internal circulation system.

Residential quarters in inner-city areas were densely built up; houses were more closely set together, with one compound next to the other, often sharing party walls. Babylonian cities were not built to a regular grid layout like some Egyptian towns. Streets were rarely straight for long and the townscape rather resembled the warren-like lanes of a Moroccan Kasbah. As in later Islamic cities, houses were orientated to the inside rather than towards the street, presenting hermetic mud walls. In mid-first-millennium Babylon, the outer walls of houses were often stepped back to form a zigzag pattern which would have enlivened the street façade through the contrast of light and shade.

Because of the more constricted available space city houses often had several storeys, although this can only rarely be confirmed directly by excavations.[3] The agglomeration of spaces was generally more compact, which led to rooms with internal and external communication. However, many houses that have been excavated show that there was a central space (open or closed) around which secondary rooms were grouped. Urban houses also showed greater differentiation of wealth and status, especially in terms of size and amenities.[4] Some quarters in Old Babylonian Ur and Nippur, and in Neo-Babylonian Babylon for instance, had large dwellings with one main or several smaller paved courtyards, with upper storeys (made accessible by a wooden gallery or by internal steps) used for bedrooms and private rooms. On the ground floor were the reception rooms, kitchens, larders and other subsidiary spaces. Light could penetrate from a higher central tract by means of clerestory window openings or by lateral corridors open to the sky. Such houses could have bathrooms made watertight with a coating of bitumen and baked brick, as well as toilets draining into a clay cistern. Door sills and sockets made from stone were also a sign of wealth. Such patrician houses could have wells or cisterns and drainage to the main sewers outside. Many cuneiform tablets concern the sale of houses or their division after the patriarch's death. Clauses stipulate the number of rooms and the built-up area, as well as the existence of valuable timber items, such as door leafs, window frames, shutters, roof beams and columns. The dead were usually buried within the compound, beneath the floor or under a side wall, though wealthier houses could have brick vaults.

Mud brick houses can last for generations if their upkeep is not neglected and the walls are protected from rain and rising damp. Once the walls begin to crumble they cannot be repaired and need to be razed to the ground and new bricks laid on top of the old stumps. In this way the level of habitations increased slowly but surely over time and contributed to the characteristic rise of cities above the plains.

The climatic and thermal properties of thick mud brick walls are well known.[5] These walls absorb the heat of the day and give it off during the cooler nights. Windows in high positions, wind shafts and axially arranged doorways help to maximise the circulation of air. In contemporary Middle Eastern houses, plants and trees further enhance the quality of living. Archaeological evidence for internal gardens is scant, but the Old Babylonian palace at Mari, for instance, did have internal garden spaces.

The building trade was highly professional in Babylonia. There were brick makers and brick-layers, plasterers and carpenters, general construction workers such as hod carriers and building labourers, as well as site supervisors, surveyors and architect builders (*itinnu* or Neo-Babylonian *arad ekalli*).[6] In the Code of Hammurabi is a section that deals with the professional liabilities of the *itinnu*. Having fixed the fee as proportionate to floor space the next clause stipulates that should a man be killed when the house collapsed because of the faulty construction, the builder should be killed too, or his son or slave if the occupier's son or slave had been affected. Furthermore,

> If it has destroyed goods, he shall make good whatever was destroyed; also because he did not make the house strong which he built and it collapsed, he shall reconstruct the house which collapsed at his own expense.[7]

Because of such responsibilities the training of an architect–contractor was a lengthy process which could last up to seven years. Examples of written and drawn study exercises have survived. The most prestigious commissions were works for the great institutions, such as renovations of temples and palaces, for they were well remunerated.[8]

FURNITURE AND DOMESTIC INVENTORIES

The archaeological evidence for Babylonian furniture and household items is not extensive. Unlike the Egyptians, the Babylonians did not furnish their tombs with a complete set of equipment since they did not believe that life after death could replicate that on earth. The dead were given a few drinking vessels and some personal jewellery but sumptuous grave-goods such as those discovered in the mid-second-millennium tombs at Ur, remained a one-off.[9] There are some visual depictions on seals and terracottas, but the highly detailed representations such as those found in Assyrian palaces are lacking in Babylonia.

The main sources are therefore textual. We have the names of hundreds of items but little idea what they looked like and how they were made. The ever helpful lexical lists group objects and utensils according to their primary material and their function. The wood series of the list *HAR-ra=hubullu*[10] has a sub-section for furniture. This begins with chests (*pitnu*) – large and small – followed by some sixty entries for chairs. They enumerate different types and usage, as well as constituent parts. Then comes a very common type of seating implement, the stool: 'for bathing', 'portable', 'for the barber', 'for the road', 'for the seal cutter, for the metalworker, for the potter'. This is followed by foot-rests. Beds could be 'to sit on', 'to lie on', 'of reeds', 'with ox-feet', 'stuffed with wool', 'stuffed with goat hair', of 'Sumerian (type)', 'Akkadian (type)'. More items of furniture, and cross-references, are to be found in other sections of the list dealing with reed or metals.

The most essential items in a Babylonian household are frequently listed in wills. They were chests to store textiles and clothing, beds, chairs and stools. Some pictorial representations on seals and stelae, as well as terracotta plaques, show a variety of chair constructions, often with legs carved to resemble claws, paws or even ox-feet. Some miniature models of beds, made of clay, usually depicting a couple in the act of love-making,[11] show that beds were made of simple rectangular frames (Fig. 5.1).

Generally carpentry and 'cabinet-making' were highly specialised crafts and in the first millennium, probably also earlier, the Babylonians exported luxury furniture to Assyria and further abroad.[12] The most elaborate pieces were found in temples and palaces. Furniture there was made from wooden frames which could be covered with gold and inlaid with silver, precious stones as well as ivory. Only references in temple inventories and some descriptions in Assyrian royal annals, relating to items the kings donated to Babylonian temples, survive.

Other wooden items of a household, as listed in the lexical works, were those used for eating and cooking: bowls, spoons, plates – and here we also find tables, including those 'covered with ivory' and 'inlaid with ivory'. Various vessels are also listed ('for oil', 'for wine', 'for beer', 'for honey' ...), as well as ladders and steps, bowls, mortars and pestles.

Reeds and palm fronds were used to make a great variety of cheap everyday objects, from mats and screens, to boxes and containers, baskets and colanders. Even more ubiquitous was clay. The majority of plates and jars, jugs and storage and cooking vessels were made by potters on fast wheels. They were mass-produced and generally lacked the finesse and beauty of shape of the prehistoric pottery.

133

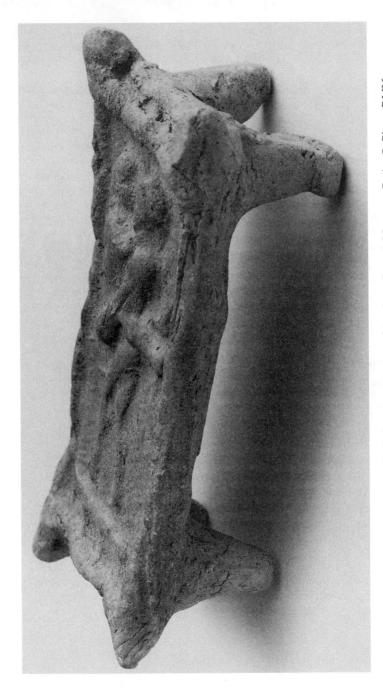

Figure 5.1 Old Babylonian clay model of a bed with a couple making love. Louvre Museum, Paris. © Photo RMN

Metal objects, especially those made of copper, often feature in the contract tablets. It appears that large cooking pots, holding between 10 and 60–70 litres (*ruqqum*) seem to have been a standard item. Metal mortars for crushing spices were also worth specifying as valuable items, as were mills and grinders made of stone.[13] In the second half of the first millennium, iron implements were introduced but they did not replace the bronze and copper household objects as there was no local expertise in working iron.

The Old Babylonian contracts make clear that while copper kettles, as well as clothing and jewellery, were primarily owned by women, any amounts of loose silver and copper, as well as furniture and items of monetary value such as stone grinders, were in the possession of men – regardless of the fact that the grinders were used primarily by women.[14]

CLOTHES, TEXTILES AND FASHION

Techniques for producing textiles have a very long history in the ancient Near East. Horizontal ground looms were in use at least since the seventh millennium and vertical, warp-weighted looms since the third millennium.[15] The main material was wool of sheep and goats; in comparison to Egypt linen was used much less, and cotton was introduced, according to an inscription by the Assyrian king Sennacherib, on an experimental basis in the seventh century.[16] Chinese silk was one of the luxury items that were imported in great quantity during the Roman period but it played little part in the Near East until Byzantine times.

The tanning of hides for leather is at least as old as the use of textiles. Leather from cattle and sheep was made into all kinds of protective garments, especially for the military and for workmen, as well as shoes and slippers.

Woollen textiles though were one of the most important products of Babylonia. Already during the time of the Third Dynasty of Ur, there were textile workshops attached to the great institutions; ration lists for the workforce consisting mainly of women and children have survived. The Assyrian merchants of the nineteenth century made healthy profits by exporting cloth and embroidered clothes to Anatolia.[17] It was often their wives who were either directly engaged in the manufacture or who supervised the female workers. According to the Mari archives there was a flourishing textile manufactory in the palace. The high-quality wool obtained from the local herds was spun and woven by female dependants or slaves acquired on military campaigns.[18] In later periods too, Babylonian textiles, including fully finished garments, were highly prized luxury items throughout the Near East.

Cloth was dyed with plant and mineral substances and the colours fixed with a variety of mordants but it is still unclear exactly which plants were used for this purpose. The high water level in Mesopotamia has not been helpful in preserving any samples of ancient cloth. At the most there is occasionally an imprint or calcinated remains of tiny fragments, so we do not know what textures, colours and finish the Babylonian textiles really had. Embroidery techniques and appliqué were also much used, as well as quilting, as the cuneiform tablets specify.

Babylonian houses and certainly palaces and temple interiors were decorated with all kinds of fabric, in the form of tapestries and wall hangings, as well as curtain-like drapes, baldachins and cushions. While simpler households laid reed mats on the floor, wealthier people would walk and sit on carpets. Some of the love lyrics specify that the couple made love on 'beds of delight' covered with bleached white sheets. The bare mud brick walls which look so drab in the excavated ruin sites must have presented a much prettier aspect when covered with fine plaster and hung with patterned cloth.

As far as Babylonian fashion is concerned, again we know the names of a number of garments and cuts, but it is often impossible to imagine what they looked like. Visual representations depict mainly deities who in any culture sport exceedingly conservative styles. The robes worn by kings and notables, as represented on seals or stelae, may also be ceremonial garb rather than everyday wear. Long fringed cloaks, with the corner tucked under the armpit – as sported by the statues of Gudea, the ruler of Lagash – were popular in the third millennium but worn by notables in the Old Babylonian period. Thus one gets the impression, which is perhaps quite wrong, that clothing styles in Babylonia changed only little over the centuries.

Generally clothes were of two kinds, tailored ones and those made of loose cloth wrapped or pinned around the body. For much of the

Babylonian period, tailored and loose clothes were worn in various combinations. Men could wear knee-length skirts or kilts and drape a piece of cloth around the torso, or wear a full-length dress with rounded collar, rather like a djellaba, with a long or short cloak. Women wore similar combinations: long, sleeved or sleeveless dresses underneath with cloaks around the shoulders. Fashion changes did not affect so much the basic cut of garments as mainly the decorations. There were flounces and fringes, which could be placed on the long edges or the hem of the dress, in single or double rows. Appliqué and embroidery could greatly enhance an outfit. The correspondence, especially of princes, proves that they were expecting high standards and keen to wear the latest fashion. Accessories were very important; belts and sashes in all kinds of material, jewellery and of course hats. Professionals could be recognised by their characteristic head-gear. There was a great variety of close-fitting caps, skull-caps, turbans, fez-like hats and conical hats, with streamers (as worn by the Babylonian kings on some stelae), and without. Women wore ribbons and circlets, as well as cap-like head-dresses and veils. In Assyria, married women had to wear a veil in public but Babylonian women were under no such legal restrictions although decorum may have demanded respectable women to cover their hair. Both men and women wore jewellery, such as rings and armbands, and officials of course wore their cylinder seal, either around the neck or on a belt. It was also part of male attire to wear a dagger-like knife.

While most people went barefoot, the better-off wore sandals and slippers. Herodotus, who claims to have visited Babylon in the fifth century, remarks that the Babylonians like to wear canes when they walk about town. There were carved at the top into 'a rose or lily or eagle or something of the sort'.[19] In the late period, new styles of clothes were introduced by the Greeks and Persians. Like in other parts of the Near East, some local people would have adopted such new fashions while others rejected them as 'foreign'.

PERSONAL APPEARANCE AND HYGIENE

Hairstyles and beards indicated status, current fashions and even social and professional groups. Unlike the Egyptians who preferred to keep their heads shaved and sport wigs in public, the Babylonians preferred to keep their natural hair. Slaves had to wear a distinctive hairstyle (*abuttu*) that could be removed on manumission; certain classes of purification priests were always clean-shaven in face and head, if not totally depilated; others, such as cult-actors (*kurgarru*), wore their hair loose and long. On an Old Babylonian mural, men wear short chin beards and short hair,[20] while a Kassite official from a fourteenth-century wall painting sports a long and carefully combed Assyrian-style 'spade beard' with his hair flowing down to his shoulders.[21] The long hair could be held back from the face by a band worn across the forehead, as shown by the beneficiary on the seventh-century kudurru of Marduk-apla-iddina.[22]

There are no representations of females in an official setting.[23] Goddesses are shown often with flounced robes or a tight-fitting dress, as worn by the statue from Mari of the goddess holding a water vessel; her hair falls onto her shoulder from beneath a horned cap, the symbol of divinity.[24] Old Babylonian terracotta plaques or statuettes, which belong to a much more informal art tradition, depict women with long hair parted in the middle, or partially plaited and woven around the head (Fig. 5.2). Chignons, popular in the Sumerian period, were apparently worn much less by the Babylonians.

As far as body care is concerned, we need to look at literary and omen texts, as well as proverbs; the lexical lists give us an insight into items of toiletry. Babylonians of all classes washed frequently as the numerous references to bathing and washing testify. This was done as much for physical comfort and the removal of the ever present dust, as for a wish to remove any contagion by evil influences. Many of the upper-class houses had special bathrooms and in-built toilets. On entering a house, visitors were given a basin to wash their feet and it was mandatory to wash one's hands before eating. An amorous woman prepared for her lover by bathing with 'pure soap' and anointing her body with fragrant oils.[25] According to Sumerian literary compositions, people could also bathe in the canals, among the reeds, which made young girls prone to be sexually molested.[26]

In the Epic of Gilgamesh, the whole narrative is punctuated by a contrast between bodily cleanliness and the wearing of clothes and dirt and the donning of animal hides. 'Wild man' Enkidu, created by the gods as a companion to Gilgamesh, the king of Uruk, was roaming the desert, like a beast covered in shaggy hair. He is

Figure 5.2 Painted terracotta bust of a woman, perhaps a dedication to a temple, c. 1900 BC. The hair is worn held back by a ribbon at the forehead, parted in the middle, with looped braids on either side. (© British Museum)

made human by having sex with a voluptuous prostitute from the city. Thereafter the animals turn away from him, since 'his body was too clean' (Tablet I, iv: 26). The Old Babylonian version is even more specific about his transformation into a human being: he is given food 'the symbol of life' and beer 'destiny of the land' to drink, then he anoints himself with oil 'and (to) become like any man, he put on clothes' (Tablet II, iii). Gilgamesh undergoes the process in the opposite way after the death of Enkidu – his appearance is wasted and 'clad only in a lion skin' he flees the city. The Old Babylonian version includes a passage where the Ale Wife 'who lives down by the sea' advises the grief-stricken hero to give up his futile quest for eternal life and to enjoy life's simple pleasures while they last:

> Day and night, dance and play,
> Wear fresh clothes.
> Keep your head washed, bathe in water,
> Appreciate the child who holds your hand,
> Let your wife enjoy herself in your lap.[27]

Cleanliness was also seen as a prerequisite for a general state of purity and in Enkidu's cursing of his temptress degradation is associated with dirt and the absence of cosmetics:

> Filth shall impregnate your lovely lap, the drunkard
> shall soak your party dress with vomit
> [   ] fingers(?)
> [your cosmetic paint (?) shall be] the potter's lump of
> clay (?)
> You shall never obtain the best cosmetic [oil (?),][28]

The late version, preserved on the copies from Ashurbanipal's library, contains injunctions as to how to behave in the underworld:

> [You must not put on] a clean garment,
> For they will recognise that you are a stranger.
> You must not be anointed with perfumed oil from an
> ointment jar,
> For they will gather around you at the smell of it.
>
> (Tablet XII, i)

The most interesting passage, however, from the same edition, occurs in Tablet XI, when Gilgamesh, as a consolation for his failure to obtain 'eternal life', is given a plant called 'an old man grows into a young man' which the hero takes with him on his return journey to Uruk. As he stops for the night, he sees

A pool whose water was cool,
And went down into the water and washed.
A snake smelt the fragrance of the plant,
It came up silently and carried off the plant,
As it took it away, it shed its scaly skin.

(Tablet XI, vi)

Thus the creature associated with death and the underworld obtains the secret to rejuvenate; it is lost to mankind precisely because of the desire for purity.

Some of the above quotes referred to fragrant ointments. While the Babylonians did not use oil as a cleansing agent like the Greeks, they anointed themselves with oils made fragrant by infusing flowers and aromatic resins. An Assyrian recipe from the late second millennium specifies that plants such as myrtle had, for some days, to be steeped in water which was then skimmed. The infusion was mixed with oil.[29] Temples and even houses were made fragrant by burning aromatic wood and resins, as much to ward off evil influences as to make the dwelling pleasant.

In addition to their taste for frequent ablutions, clean clothes and careful grooming of hair and beard, the Babylonians, especially but not exclusively the women, liked to complete their toilette with cosmetics. Stone, ivory or metal palettes were much coveted luxury items, and could be beautifully finished. As among tribal Arabs of today, bright eyes were accentuated by applying black antimony paste (Arabic kohl) around the eyelids. Blue and green eye shadow were obtained from minerals such as cobalt and malachite. Such adornment was thought to make the wearer more attractive to the opposite sex, as some of the 'brand names' – such as 'May He Come' – indicate. Rouge, probably made from ochre, was applied to lips and cheeks.

There is no evidence that other body decorations, such as tattooing or scarification, were practised by the Babylonians. Nor is there any mention of males (let alone females) being circumcised.

FOOD AND DRINK

An adequate supply of food and drink was seen as one of the most important achievements of the Mesopotamian urban civilisation.

We have seen how wild man Enkidu became human after he ate bread and drank beer. The nomadic people were despised because of what was considered their barbarous dietary habits – the eating of 'raw meat' and 'not knowing bread'. The daily sacrifices offered to deities were huge meals accompanied by copious drink; these were subsequently distributed among the temple staff. The topic of divine banquets frequently occurs in myths and proverbial sayings and underlines the social function of shared eating and drinking:

> Give food to eat, beer to drink,
> Grant what is asked, provide for and honour.
> In this a man's god takes pleasure.[30]

Since most of the agricultural production was maintained and organised by the large institutions who also had control over the necessary machinery and draught animals, as well as store-houses for surplus produce, the food supply in Babylonia was less fraught than in societies which relied on smallholders or private estates, as in classical Rome for instance. The most important crop were cereals, especially the salt-tolerant barley.[31] In the first millennium, dates from large-scale date-palm plantations became second in importance to the grain staple. Protein was obtained primarily from pulses. Like the Egyptian lentil stew beloved by Israelites in Exodus, dishes made from chickpeas, beans and lentils were a staple. These legumes were grown on small plots between the cornfields for the needs of individual families.

The administrative texts of temples and palaces also refer to substantial livestock holdings. Sheep and goats, as well as cattle, were kept for meat, wool, leather and dairy products. The last were appropriate to the hot climate: clarified butter rather than fresh, fermented milk (a sort of yoghurt), and a variety of cheeses some of which could be reconstituted in water. Meat was regularly served to the gods and formed part of the meals consumed by the more senior-ranking temple staff. Food from the king's table or the 'palace' was also rich in a variety of meat dishes, including game, and some of this was also distributed to a wider group of diners. Sheep and goat, cattle and pigs were eaten, as were deer and fowl, mainly ducks and geese (chickens were introduced much later). The general populace probably did not eat meat on a daily basis and the basic rations only comprise of barley, oil and beer. Vitamins were supplied mainly by onions and garlic, leeks, and herbs such as coriander. Babylonian food was one of the ancestors of the later Middle Eastern cuisine; naturally without any of the 'new world' foods – tomatoes, maize, potatoes and peppers were brought to the Middle East only in the fifteenth century AD. Gourds and pumpkins were popular; they grew well in the vicinity of irrigation ditches, as did cucumbers and (cos) lettuces. Dates, fresh or dried, were a rich source of minerals, vitamins and sugar. The fruits could also be fermented to make a sweet alcoholic drink, confusingly also called 'beer'. Even the crushed stones were a valuable supplementary feed for cattle. Date-palms were by far the most important fruit trees in Babylonia. In a literary Dialogue between the Tamarisk and Date-palm, the latter sings its own praise:

> You tamarisk are a useless tree,
> what are your branches? Wood without fruit!
> My fruit ....
> .... second..
> The gardener speaks well of me,
> A benefit to both slave and magistrate.
> .. my fruit makes the baby grow,
> Grown men eat my fruit.
> .. the equal of the king....[32]

Other fruit trees were figs and pomegranates, as well as medlars (often translated as 'apricots' or 'apples'). The lexical lists refer to many other fruit-bearing trees but they are not identifiable botanically.

Oil and fat, either of vegetable origin such as linseed or sesame, or in the form of lard and butter, were important for cooking. Vegetable oil formed part of the rations and was therefore more readily available and cheaper than the animal-derived fats.

In addition to cultivated food stuffs there were also the wild resources of the rivers, canals and marshes of Babylonia, as well as the semi-desert beyond the fields. The former supplied fish and shellfish, tortoises and water-fowl. Fish were dried and one of the most popular condiments was a fermented fish sauce that gave flavour to many dishes. The semi-desert was rich in wild-life, such as gazelles and deer, and locusts – a delicacy, grilled or pickled. Other wild food were bulbs and tubers, mushrooms and bee honey. In addition to these locally grown or produced food items, there was imported food from the north, especially nuts, raisins and wine from Syria.

As far as drink was concerned, the Babylonians were beer drinkers. There was a general divide in the Ancient Near East between barley eaters and beer drinkers, and wheat eaters and wine drinkers. The latter lived in the regions at or near the Mediterranean coast. Wine was by no means unknown in Mesopotamia, but it remained an imported luxury item only to be found on the tables of the elite. Wealthy patrons could choose among many different types of wine, both red and white, sweet and dry, young and aged, and from different wine-producing regions of the Near East.

The indigenous drink of Babylonia was beer, which came in many different degrees of strength and quality. In the second millennium most beer was made from malted barley; in the first millennium date beer seems to have become more widely brewed when the cultivation of barley declined. Barley grain was well watered and left to sprout. The resulting sugar-rich malt was then dried and ground. To this meal one added 'beer bread', containing yeast from leaven, and enough water to form a dough which was baked into cakes. In this form they could be stored and transported and were ready for brewing. All that was needed now was enough fresh water to cover the dried mixture in a large vessel and to let it ferment. The dregs dripped through a hole at the bottom and the beer was ready for drinking.[33] The lexical texts again give us the nomenclature for many different types of beer, with different degrees of quality and presumably alcohol content. Beer was both nutritious, due to the malt, and rich in vitamins and minerals. Since particular care was taken to ensure that the water used for brewing was clean, it was generally safer to drink beer than the water from nearby canals. As such it contributed substantially to the general well-being of the working population, combining nutritional value with a safe source of liquid, all with the added benefit of the mood-enhancing properties of alcohol.

On the whole, the Babylonian texts give the impression that a wide variety of food was generally available. It has been calculated that the calories supplied by the most standard rations of beer and barley exceed those advocated by the United Nations in modern times.

However, while such a desirable state of affairs may have been the norm rather than the exception for many centuries, it was by no means guaranteed. Even the best management can lead to over-production and increased salinity because of over-irrigation, and when the rivers changed their course or the waterways became blocked as a result of neglect in times of war and civil disruption, severe problems could arise. These situations are vividly described in literary texts such as the Babylonian Flood Epic, the *Atrahasis*. After the gods had created mankind to alleviate the junior gods from the labour, they found their peace and sleep disturbed by the ceaseless noise of human beings. One attempt to diminish the number of people was to cut off their food:

> Let vegetation be too scant for their stomachs!
> Let Adad on high make his rain scarce,
> Let him block below, and not raise flood-water from the springs!
> Let the field decrease its yields,
> Let Nisaba turn away her breast,
> Let the dark fields become white,
> Let the broad countryside breed alkali
> Let the earth down her womb
> So that no vegetation sprouts, no grain grows,
> Let ašakku[34] be inflicted on the people
> Let the womb be too tight to let a baby out![35]
> (....)
> When the second year arrived
> They had depleted the storehouse.
> When the third year arrived
> People's looks were changed [by starvation].
> When the fourth year arrived
> Their upstanding bearing bowed
> Their well-set shoulders slouched, people went out in
> public hunched over, when the fifth year arrived
> A daughter would eye her mother coming in, a mother
> would not even open her door to her daughter,
> A daughter would watch the scales (at the sale of her mother)
> A mother would watch the scales at the (sale of her) daughter,
> When the sixth year arrived,

They served up a daughter for a meal,
Served up a son for food.[36]

This passage describes the gradual physical and moral decay of the starving population, after the fields had turned white from salt and alkali and the storehouses could not be replenished by new harvests. Environmental archaeologists have documented the exhaustion of the arable land at certain periods. Nippur for instance, was almost deserted for generations at the end of the Old Babylonian period.[37]

COOKING

Babylonian cooking techniques were manifold,[38] as the cuneiform documents relating to food preparation and the archaeological record of surviving pottery and vessels indicate. Most houses had their own *tinuru* or dome-shaped clay oven still found in Middle Eastern villages to this day. Meat cut in small cubes could be grilled directly over the open flame; larger households also had specially constructed ovens that allowed steam cooking. This was used to bake flat leavened bread, like the Arabic *hubs*. We have seen that the most common household item was the large, flat-bottomed kettle *(ruqqu)*, used to boil food in water over an open fire. Hand mills and mortars for the crushing of grain were also part of the standard equipment. Barley was eaten in the form of porridge or mush, and mortars were also needed to crush garlic and flavourings. The range of cooking facilities, serving dishes and eating utensils varied with people's social status and material wealth. The large institutions and wealthy elite families could command a large kitchen staff. Like in many other stratified societies the degree of sophistication in preparation of food rose in proportion to status and income. In an average family, it was the women who were responsible for the daily meals and it was up to their ingenuity to vary the daily fare which consisted of the staples, such as barley, pulses and onions.

A temple household or the palace not only had many more hands in the kitchen but also could employ male overseers or chefs *(muhatimmu)* who were experts of their craft. The lexical lists have preserved some 800 entries for food items, listing 100 different soups, 300 kinds of bread defined by their flavouring, filling and shape ('large', 'small', 'tiny', 'like an ear', 'like a woman's breast'). The Babylonians were well aware that cooking represents one of the most fundamental aspects of one's culture and as such they made an effort to preserve or perhaps codify their culinary knowledge, much as they did their other forms of expertise, like omen interpretation or astronomy. Only relatively few texts have been identified as such so far. The best known are three tablets, containing 35 recipes, kept at the Yale Babylonian Collection, and dating from around 1700. They have been edited and translated by the French scholar Jean Bottéro.[39] The three tablets do not comprise a Babylonian kitchen manual and constitute only a small part of known cooking techniques since they deal only with meat dishes cooked in a liquid medium ('bouillons' and sauces). Perhaps the ancient authors chose this particular field of repertoire because cooking food slowly in a liquid enriched with a variety of ingredients represents, as Bottéro indicates, a 'true cuisine, with all its complexities ands its studied refinements'.[40] Its antithesis is simple roasting or grilling, a much more archaic technique, and as such suitable for ritual offerings.

The Yale recipes show that the act of boiling meat was indeed a complex operation which could involve several stages and changes of cooking pots. Meat was seared first, then heated again in a small amount of liquid. Next it was boiled for a long time in water to which fat had been added, which adds flavour and raises the cooking temperature. The composition of the stock was a matter of great importance, showing the true culinary art. Offal, extremities, and other secondary cuts of one or several kinds of animal were added, having been seared and washed first. Other ingredients – vegetables, minerals and processed or bottled preparations (such as the fermented fish sauce) – imparted different tastes. Some dishes have forty different additives, and many cannot be identified. Some of these were added whole, others were ground to a powder, or soaked in beer or milk first. Certain ingredients were cooked with the meat added at the start, others added at later stages or at the end. Garlic or leeks were essential items. Bottéro noticed that a number of condiments also appear in pairs, as if to complement and balance each other in a particular way. When the dish was finally ready to be presented, it was accompanied by fresh greens, fresh garlic, salt and vinegar, and with some of the cooking stock as a sauce. Further garnishes were grain porridges, and the meat itself could be laid on a pastry crust made from different types of dough. It is clear that not only was the nutritious value of the food considered, as well as the right consistency and tenderness of the meat, and the subtle and rich blend of flavours, but that fanciful presentation mattered as much. Below is a recipe for a pigeon dish:

> The animal having been sacrificed, it is plucked after it was plunged into hot water. Once plucked, it is washed in cold water and one severs the neck, leaving the fleshy skin on, and cuts off the sides. Wash the body, and leave it in cold water. Chop the gizzard from which the outer membrane has been removed. Open and finely chop the intestines.
>
> For the boiling in the pot, one puts into a cauldron the body, gizzard, intestines, and head (of the pigeon), as well as a piece of mutton and put it on the fire. Take off the fire, rinse everything carefully in plenty of cold water and wipe dry with care. Sprinkle with salt and put it into a pot. Cover with water and add: a piece of de-veined fat, vinegar and [....], *samidu*, leek and crushed garlic, onions, and if necessary some more water. One lets it simmer.
>
> Once it is cooked, one pounds and crushes together in order to add it (to the stew): leek, garlic, *andahsu* and *kisimmu*, or in default of that crushed and pounded *baru*. Then one wipes the pigeon taken from the pot and [   ] the oven of which one pushes the heat to roast (?) a high fire the legs, which have first been wrapped in dough. Add the fillets (?) until [   ].
>
> When all is cooked, one takes the meat off the fire, and before the stock has become lukewarm (?), it is served, accompanied by garlic, greenery and vinegar. The stock can be eaten first or served as a side dish. It is ready to be served.[41]

HEALTH AND MEDICINE

Although we have seen that the diet of the average Babylonian was adequate in terms of calories and vitamins, and that basic hygiene measures were not unknown, people's health could be affected in a number of ways. First of all, in the densely populated cities pathogens were quickly spread. Refuse was thrown over the walls to rot in the streets and canals and waterways became quickly contaminated. Several literary texts describe epidemics sweeping through cities. Stomach aches and other digestive ailments were chronic. The high temperatures of the summer months were also problematic, causing fever and exhaustion, as well as inflammation of the eyes and mucous membranes because of the ever present dust and frequent sand-storms. The cold nights of winter led to respiratory troubles, coughs and colds. Women's health was adversely affected by frequent pregnancies, and childbirth itself fraught with danger. The mothers gave birth squatting on a few bricks (the 'birth brick') and were assisted by midwives. Childhood mortality rates were high, but not significantly higher than anywhere else in the ancient world. Agricultural labour and hard physical work, such as canal dredging, resulted in work-related strain and arthritis. Really dangerous occupations, such as mining, which demanded the lives of so many Roman slaves, were not common in Babylonia.

Our knowledge about health and medicine in Mesopotamia is primarily based on written records. There were two main strands, folk medicine and institutional medicine. Common ailments were treated at home, taking recourse to traditional substances and elixirs. There are some proverbs which allude to common afflictions and their causes:

> Eat no fat and there will be no blood in your excrement.

> Has she become pregnant without intercourse? Has she become fat without eating?

> Last year I ate garlic, this year my insides burn.[42]

While a number of health problems were thus seen to have been caused by dietary habits, or the effects of the season, a more persistent illness was invariably thought to have been caused by demons or other malfarious supernatural agents. Therefore, the best prevention against disease was apotropaic and any cure had to deal with the offending agent first. The treatment of the symptoms, such as to alleviate a bad cough, was but a secondary part of the main cure. It is therefore not surprising that 'proper' medicine, in the Babylonian sense, was part of the institutional sciences of anti-demonology. The patient had to consult diviners to identify which supernatural agent was responsible in the first place and then the physician had to treat symptoms and suggest the cure. While the training of physicians (*ašu*) also took many years and required literacy, their status was lower than that of diviners, since they were not charged with the detection of the root cause.

The lexical lists have sections for parts of the human body and its organs, as well as for diseases. Furthermore, there were recipes for unguents, concoctions and infusions, listing ingredients, quantities and methods of preparation. Herbs, minerals and even metals were used in complex combinations. One famous medical text, known as *uruanna maštakal*, lists hundreds of ingredients, and was written in a deliberately cryptic style which renders it particularly obscure. Medicines were swallowed (mixed with beer or syrup), rubbed onto the body, inhaled, or inserted by means of enemas or suppositories. The ingredients were not selected as much for their effects on the body of the patient as for their more esoteric properties in relation to the Babylonian understanding of the universe. It was these hidden qualities and network of interactive forces which were of greatest interest to the Babylonian scholar. Perhaps, as a result, pragmatic medicine, based on direct observation of the body, never developed further. Nor was surgery practised, except for the most basic operations to remove obstacles.

The more elevated the status of the patient the more complex was the diagnosis and treatment of his illness. Babylonian physicians, together with their learned colleagues, the diviners, were consulted by the kings and members of the royal families of Assyria. Their letters to the kings reveal how carefully they had to proceed with such powerful clients.[43] There were endless deliberations and consultations to ensure that no possible cause was overlooked.

For less august patients, the matter was more straightforward. There is an interesting compendium of cures for impotence, for instance, called ŠÀ.ZI.GA (literally 'the rising of the heart').[44] The affected male was treated first by having an appropriate incantation recited before him:

> Incantation: Let the wind blow! Let the mountains quake!
> Let the clouds gather! Let the moisture fall! Let the ass

swell up! Let him mount the jenny! Let the buck get an
erection! Let him again and again mount the young she-
goat!
(....)
At the head of the bed I have tied a buck!
At one foot of the bed I have tied a ram!
The one at the head of the bed, get hard, make love to
me!
The one at the foot of the bed, get hard. Make love to me!
My vagina is the vagina of a bitch. His penis is the penis
of a dog,
as the vagina of the bitch holds fast the penis of the dog,
(so may my vagina hold fast his penis!)[45]

Here the incantation alone, uttered as though by a woman, was
meant to effectuate at least a temporary cure of the afflicted organ
through the vivid imagery of the spell which in the original sounds
rather less clinical than the translation here suggests. The treatment is completed by the following ritual:

'Its ritual: pulverised magnetic iron ore, pulverised iron,
you put into puru-oil, recite the incantation over it seven
times. The man rubs his penis, the woman her vulva (with
this oil), then he can have intercourse.[46]

The hardness of the iron is magically transferred to the organ which
should respond to the physical application and the psychological
stimulation. These examples illustrate the attitude of pragmatism
combined with magic which must have been quite effective.

BABYLONIAN SEXUALITY

The context also invites some comments on Babylonian sexual
mores. The sources are not very plentiful for this subject; there are
only a few pictorial scenes which show copulating (heterosexual)
couples, generally on a bed, some standing up.[47] Many hundreds
of terracotta figurines depicting nude females have been found in
all sorts of archaeological contexts, including tombs. They are often

shown supporting their breasts. It is not clear what they represented to the Babylonians, whether they were seen as love charms,
symbols of fertility, or whether they were the equivalent of Pirelli
calendar girls. Love poetry with strongly erotic language was not
unknown; here is an Old Babylonian example:

> Rise and let me make love to you,
> in your delicious lap, the one for love-making,
> your passion is sweet.
> Growing luxuriantly is your 'fruit'.
> My bed of incense is *ballukku* perfumed,
> O by the crown of our head, the rings of our ears,
> the hills of our shoulders, the voluptuousness of our
> breast,
> the bracelet of our wrists
> the belt of our waist,
> reach out (and) with your left hand to touch our vulva,
> Fondle our breasts!
> Enter, I have opened my thighs (..)[48]

The context of this passionate address is unfortunately unknown.
There is a tantalising catalogue of love songs, listing the titles, but
few of the actual verses are preserved.[49] Some of the narrative literature deals with themes of sexual attraction, so for instance the
myth of Nergal and Ereshkigal, and to some extent the Gilgamesh
Epic where there is a strong homoerotic tenor to the friendship
between Enkidu and Gilgamesh, although this may have been
understood differently by the Babylonians. The Old Babylonian
version contains the advice by Siduri that men should enjoy life's
pleasures and rejoice in the conjugal embrace. Male homosexuality
was not unknown but the passive partner was despised; at least this
is the impression we get from the omens that deal with unusual
sexual behaviour.[50] They also refer to anal intercourse and sex with
such women who were apparently not supposed to have any sexual
relations. Generally, Babylonian women, living in a patriarchal
society, were bound to their husbands. They were married at a
young age and were not supposed to have had sexual experience
beforehand. Once married, a wife was expected to remain faithful
to her husband and adultery was a serious offence. At least according

to the Code of Hammurabi, a woman lying with another man could be thrown into the river, bound to her lover, although if the husband wished to pardon her the king could spare her life.[51] Since the main purpose of marriage was to produce children, a barren wife could be divorced, although her dowry had to be returned, again according to Hammurabi's Laws. The legal documents make clear that divorce was not uncommon; women could leave men who treated them badly or failed to provide for them, but they could not sue for adultery.

Herodotus' story that Babylonian women had to offer themselves to strangers in the temple forecourt is not borne out by any local sources and seems most implausible. It is more likely that prostitutes operated near or even within some temple precincts, especially that of the goddess Ishtar whose staff included a number of specialist cult practitioners who had some, still obscure connection with sexuality, 'who frequently do abominable acts to please the heart of Ishtar', according to a line in the Erra Epic. This goddess was certainly the one who presided over all aspects of sexuality; she was not revered as a mother-goddess, or even as an emblem of fertility. Although some hymns to Ishtar praise her as the lofty Lady of Heaven, she is above all

> She of joy, clothed with love, adorned with seduction,
> grace, and sex appeal,
> Honey-sweet are her lips, life is her mouth, adored in
> laughing femininity.[52]

Without her all sexual activity comes to an end, as the myth of Ishtar's Descent to the Underworld vividly describes. Life without sex was unthinkable, and many incantations against witches focus on their detrimental effects on people's sexual appetite:

> She robs the handsome man of his vitality,
> she takes the pretty girl's 'fruit',
> with her glance she steals her sex appeal.[53]

Ishtar ensured reproduction but she also embodied all other, even transgressive, aspects of sexuality. She is portrayed as a woman wild with passion who hunts for men in taverns, who steals the husband from his wife, who 'turns men into women' (a still disputed epithet, which could refer to transsexuality or homosexuality). Some of the rites at Ishtar's temples, both at Uruk and Babylon, seem to have involved highly theatrical displays by her specialist performers, such as the *kurgarru*, who dramatised episodes of Ishtar's love life, such as the already mentioned love triangle between Marduk and his wife. In comparison to the more straight-laced Assyrians, who secluded their women in harems and forbade them to appear unveiled in public, the urban Babylonians seem to have been more 'permissive'. It is quite likely that the many prostitutes, transsexual performers, and acts of more or less public copulation were shocking to people who were accustomed to more austere behaviour,[54] such as the exiled Jews, who were to pass on their impressions of the Babylonian fornication to many subsequent generations.

DEATH AND AFTERLIFE

Babylonian views on death can be gleaned from some of the literary works and from their mortuary practices. The gods reserved eternal life for themselves and decreed death to be man's fate. Man has to enjoy life on earth while it lasts, since conditions in the underworld are nothing to look forward to. According to the eleventh tablet of the Gilgamesh Epic, the spirit of Enkidu appears to Gilgamesh to say:

> If I tell you Earth's conditions that I found,
> You must sit and weep!

The former beloved wife is being eaten by vermin, the spirits 'grovel in the dust', only those with many sons (to perform funerary rites) are 'glad of heart' because they have water to drink. The fate of the unburied dead and of those who have no one to supply their offerings is more bitter; they are not even allowed to 'sleep in the Earth' and 'feed on dregs from dishes, and bits of bread that lie abandoned in the streets'. Such unfortunate beings were much feared as unhappy and vengeful ghosts who haunt the living. There are some allusions to a judgement of the dead, performed by the sun-god on his daily journey through the underworld, but this was not a notion that seems to have had general currency. The Babylonians did not believe in either retributions or rewards for one's behaviour after death. Instead, they were more inclined to interpret misfortune, illness and of course death itself as a form of punishment for 'sin'.

They grieved for the dead, lamenting their passing as Gilgamesh does in the Epic when Enkidu dies. But they accepted death as the 'fate of mankind'. They preferred to bury the deceased within the family compound, below the thick mud brick walls, or beneath the floor of a little-used room, sometimes in clay coffins, with few if any grave-goods. Thus the ancestors remained part of the house and it was convenient to offer them their daily libations of water, a duty that the male heirs performed. Death was a family affair, it did not concern the institutions. The Assyrian kings were buried in big stone sarcophagi in the royal hypogeum at Ashur but no tomb of any Babylonian king has so far been discovered.

While their attitude to death was pragmatic and they did not engage much in eschatological speculation, they were concerned with the continuity of life on earth. The most terrible and most frequently uttered curse was to 'have one's seed cut off', which implied to die without living issue. Children and grandchildren ensured that the line continued, that one's seed had born fruit. The intellectual Babylonians knew of another form of immortality, that bestowed by literary fame. They left their names and pedigree on the tablets they wrote, in the certainty that in distant days these would be read. Gilgamesh, having learned that eternal life was unobtainable, returned to his city and wrote down what he had seen. Kings, who commemorated their pious deeds on golden tablets buried in safe boxes below the foundations, confidently addressed the future kings to read their tablets with care and to treat them with respect, while those ignorant or evil enough to cast them aside should be cursed with eternal oblivion.

NOTES

ABBREVIATIONS

CAH: *Cambridge Ancient History*
MSL: *Materials for the Sumerian Lexicon*
RIA: *Reallexikon der Assyriologie*
UET: *Ur Excavation Texts*

CHAPTER 1

1 See Adams 1981, Buringh 1957, Butzer 1995, Charles 1988, Milano et al. 1999, Moorey 1994, Sanlaville 1989, Weiss 1986.
2 Leach E. 1976:51, quoted in Harley and Woodward 1987: 2.
3 Röllig W. 1980–3 'Landkarten' *Reallexikon der Assyriologie und Archäologie* 6:464–6; Millard 1987: 107–16.
4 Harley and Woodward 1987, ch. 1.
5 An exceptional geographical list from the Early Dynastic period (c. 2700) follows quite a different system by ordering cities according to their location along ancient canals. Frayne 1992: 3. This hypothesis is difficult to verify because it is impossible to know where most of the places mentioned actually were.
6 Landsberger 1974.
7 Usually beginning with Nippur, Ur, Uruk, Isin, Sippar . . .
8 E.g. 'land', Sumer, Akkad, Subartu, Gutium (MSL XI:55).
9 Way station, tavern, 'house of Gula' (hospital), palace, palace of the crown-prince . . . (MSL XI:14).
10 E.g. cedar-mountain, Marhashu Mt., Assyrian mountain, Elamite mountain, Gutian mountain . . . (MSL XI:14).
11 Beginning with Tigris and Euphrates.
12 In one literary text, known as the *Sargon Geography*, the entire earth's surface is equated with the empire of Sargon, including all of Assyria and Babylonia, the eastern countries of Elam, Anshan and Marhashi (all in present-day Iran), the lands along the Euphrates to the Cedar

Mountain, as well as further west, the regions right up to the Mediterranean coast, and the 'Upper Sea'. See Horowitz 1998: 67–95. The text is thought to have been composed in the Neo-Assyrian period, perhaps by one of Sargon II successors, Sennacherib or Esarhaddon.

13 Horowitz 1998.

14 According to another text (KAR 307) the earth is divided into three regions: upper earth being the earth's surface (where human beings live), middle earth being the Apsu and home of the god Ea, and lower earth being the underworld where the dead live. Horowitz 1998: 318.

15 Heinrich and Seidl 1967.

16 However, on a sixth-century temple plan which seems to be in scale, in the ratio of 1:66 and 2/3, see Heinrich and Seidl 1967: 42 note 9.

17 Kramer and Bernhardt 1970; also Kramer 1981: 375–9.

18 Röllig RlA 6:465.

19 Horowitz 1998: 20–42.

20 Horowitz 1998: 151.

21 Algaze 1993. For the writing system see Nissen, Damerow and Englund 1993, Schmandt-Besserat 1992.

22 See Walker 1987.

23 Driver 1976, Healey 1990.

24 Folmer 1995.

25 Pearce 1993: 188.

CHAPTER 2

1 See Aström 1987–9, Brinkman J.A. in Oppenheim 1977: 335–48, and more recently Gasche et al. 1998.

2 First devised by Christian Thompson in 1816–19; the use of iron follows that of bronze which follows that of stone.

3 This scheme is used, though in conjunction with more conventional chronologies, in Hallo and Simpson 1998.

4 See Pollock 1999, Charvát 2002, Leick 2001: chapter 2.

5 For a general discussion of this period see Liverani 1993: 69–90.

6 Here is an excerpt from a royal inscription by Rimush, Sargon's son and successor who faced widespread revolts: 'Thereupon, on his return, Kuzallu revolted. He conquered it and [wi]thin Kuzallu (itself) struck down 12,052 men. He took 5,862 captives. Further, he captured Asared, governor of Kuzallu, and destroyed its (Kuzallu's) wall' (see Frayne 1993: 48, lines 44–63).

7 According to the scheme of the Sumerian King List there had been two other dynasties at Ur during the first half of the third millennium, the so-called Early Dynastic Period. The famous Royal Graves, which Sir Leonard Woolley had excavated, date from the time of the First Ur Dynasty. For a discussion of the social structure, administration and economy of the UrIII period, see articles in Gibson and Biggs 1987; for the history, see Kuhrt 1995: 56–73.

8 It is unlikely that this extended to oral communication.

9 They are first mentioned in an inscription by the Akkadian king Shar-kali-sharri (c. 2223–2198).

10 See Buccellati 1966.

11 Kraus 1974: 253.

12 So Nissen 1988: 131.

13 The land in the southern plains is only about 20m above sea level which leads to high levels of salinity if the irrigation water is not drained off sufficiently. See also Jacobsen 1982.

14 Postgate 1992: 83.

15 For an investigation of an Old Babylonian neighbourhood using ethnographic and archaeological data, see Stone 1987.

16 See for instance the hymn of Iddin-Dagan, in Reisman 1973.

17 Sommerfeld in Sasson 1995: 928.

18 See L. Woolley 1927 *Antiquaries Journal* VII and Stone 1987.

19 This is the date given in most publications. For a later date see Gasche et al. 1998.

20 Gasche et al. 1998.

21 See Brinkman J.A. 1980 *Reallexikon der Assyriologie und Archäologie* vol. V:468; see generally *Cambridge Ancient History* vol. III, Kuhrt 1995.

22 Lambert 1971, Brinkman J.A. 1980 *Reallexikon der Assyriologie und Archäologie* vol. V:468.

23 Moran 1992.

24 See Zaccagini G. 'The Interdependence of the Great Powers' in Cohen and Westbrook 2000: 141–53.

25 See Zettler 1992, Brinkman 1968.

26 Brinkman J.A. 1999 *Reallexikon der Assyriologie und Archäologie* 9:192–3.

27 See Schwartz 1989.

28 See Neuman and Parpola 1987.

29 There has been some speculation that this was a throne name for Ashurbanipal himself (CAH III ch. 25) but the existence of a Babylonian governor alongside Kandalanu makes this unlikely (Kuhrt 1995: 589).

30 See Borger 1965, Berger 1973; Wiseman D.J. 1991 'Babylonia 605–539 BC' *Cambridge Ancient History* 3.2:229–51.

31 Lambert 1965, Streck M. 1999 in *Reallexikon der Assyriologie und Archäologie* 9:194–201.

32 Koldewey 1990.

33 Beaulieu 1989, 1995; Sack 1983, Dandamaev M. 1998 *Reallexikon der Assyriologie und Archäologie* 9:6–11.

34 Pointed out some time ago by Funk 1982: 67, n. 63.

35 See Kuhrt 1987.

36 See, for instance, Doty 1977.

CHAPTER 3

1 A bilingual proverb, Lambert 1960: Proverbs IV: 14–21, translation p. 232.
2 Such cases are known mainly from mid-first millennium Babylon and Uruk.
3 See, for instance, Oppenheim 1967.
4 Diakonoff 1965, 1972, 1982; Dandamayev 1984, 1988.
5 As proposed by Gelb 1979: 5.
6 See Kraus 1969.
7 See Tsukimoto 1985.
8 On temple organisation, see Chapter 4.
9 See, for instance, Stone and Owen 1991.
10 To what extent this affected only the better-off social groups – as was the case in Europe's Middle Ages – is not known since written marriage contracts were drawn up only for wealthier families.
11 UET 5:49 lists 1 1/2 kilogram of silver, five slaves, three tables, two copper kettles, one copper bowl, ten bronze vessels, two bronze mirrors, two storage vessels, two pestles, four chairs, one bed and ten spoons, Mieroop 1992: 218.
12 Column iii 12–13, Dalley 1989: 150.
13 For instance, 'Quiet Street' was the name given by the excavator Sir Leonard Woolley who used the topography of central Oxford as a source for naming the streets of Ur. He suspected that this street was perhaps like a 'cathedral close'; see Woolley 1954: 175 and the detailed study by Charpin 1986: 140–1 who substantiated the assumption, pointing out some shortcomings of Woolley's analogy since the houses inhabited by the temple staff were owned by them and not the temple. For a similar cluster (at Ur) of businessmen, see the section below on entrepreneurs.
14 So Jongman W. 'Theories, Models and Methods in Roman Economic History' in Bongenaar 2000: 269, also Parkin T.G. 1992 *Demography and Roman Society* (Baltimore).
15 Jongman 'Theories' 269.
16 Four oxen were the norm in the first millennium.
17 Such yields were less easily obtained in the Babylonian periods, because of over-production, salinity of fields and general decline of fertility. In the first millennium intensive date-palm cultivation to some extent off-set such shortfalls, see van Driel 2000: 11.
18 For the Neo-Babylonian period, see Joannès F. 'Relations entre intérets privés et biens des sanctuaires' in Bongenaar 2000: 25–41.
19 See Sigrist 1984, Sigrist 1977 èš-ta-gur-ra, *Révue d'Assyriologie* 71:117–24.
20 Mieroop 1992: 105.
21 So G. van Driel 'Capital Formation and Investment' in Dercksen 1999: 28.
22 Ibid. 11.

23 See, for instance, the donation of Egyptian slaves to the temple at Sippar following the military campaigns of Nebuchadnezzar II: Bongenaar and Haring 1994.

24 The Tamarisk and the Palmtree, lines 1–5, in Lambert 1960: 155.

25 Perhaps most so in the UrIII period and the time of Hammurabi.

26 So Renger J. 'Das Palastgeschäft in der altbabylonischen Zeit' in Bongenaar 2000: 153.

27 See Renger 'Das Palastgeschäft' for the Old Babylonian period.

28 From a hymn to the sun god Shamash, in Lambert 1960: 135, lines 138–40.

29 For a discussion of the ideological interpretations of the market economy in Mesopotamia, see Snell 1999: 145–57. In respect to the Marxist-inspired theories see Polyani K. 'Marketless Trading in Hammurabi's Time' in Polyani, Arensberg and Pearson 1957: 64–94; also Powell M.A. 'Monies, Motives and Methods in Babylonian Economics' in Dercksen 1999: 14–18.

30 For a recent summary, see Dercksen 1999.

31 The word was also used for commercial centres without a real harbour, such as those founded by the Assyrian merchants active in Anatolia.

32 Dercksen 1996; Larsen 1967.

33 Lambert 1960: 133.

34 See, however, Leemans 1950 and 1960.

35 So Joannès in Bongenaar 2000: 185.

36 See Harris 1961.

37 See Joannès F. 'Structures et opérations commerciales en Babylonie' in Dercksen 1999: 177–9, also 184–5.

38 Mieroop 1992: 114.

39 See Mieroop 1992: 132–6.

40 Mieroop 1992: 95.

41 As well as other metals, such as tin, bronze, copper and lead, and later gold. See Powell M.A. 'Monies, Motives and Methods in Babylonian Economics' in Dercksen 1999: 14–18. Powell also points out that silver was not in very wide circulation and was only used for the purchase of commodities above a certain level (a shekel of silver was a month's payment in the Old Babylonian period). Money was not used in the way it is today but functioned as 'highrange' money only. The absence of silver mines in the country also meant that the price of silver remained high throughout Mesopotamian history; see also Bongenaar A.C.V.M. 1999 'Money in the Neo-Babylonian Institutions' in Dercksen 1999: 159–74, esp. p. 174.

42 Loans were not made on an annual basis because lunar years were not of equal length.

43 Mieroop 1992: 132–6.

44 See, for instance, Krecher 1970, Wunsch 1993.

45 See Wunsch 1993; also the article by Beaulieu P.A. 'A Family of
Entrepreneurs in Neo-Babylonian Larsa' in Bongenaar 2000: 43–72
on the 'firm' of Itti-Shamash-balatu and his son Arad-Shamash 'who
leased and cultivated land from the Eanna temple, hired farm labourers
to cultivate it and kept parts of the yield as profit. They also provided
credit against pledges of land for royal workmen or soldiers obliged
to fulfill their obligations to the crown. (...) became involved in administration of the Sealand province, in trading of commodities (...) and
later probably became tax farmers, specifically tithe collectors, for the
Ebabbar temple in Larsa' (p. 62).

46 Stolper 1985.

47 See van Driel 2000.

48 see Funk B. 'Studien zur sozialökonomischen Situation Babyloniens
im 7. und 6. Jahrhundert v.u.Z.' in Klengel 1982 on the origins of
the Egibi family and that of the career of Kudurru who came to the
capital Babylon from the provinces and managed to prosper among
the metropolitan businessmen.

49 Mieroop 1992: 155.

50 Mieroop 1992: 216.

51 See Joannès F. 1992 'Inventaire d'un cabaret' NABU 1992: nos. 64
and 89.

52 After Lambert 1960: 133, lines 112–21.

53 See Gesche 2000, Pearce L. 1995 'Scribes and Scholars of Ancient
Mesopotamia' in Sasson 1995 vol. IV: 2265–78, Sjöberg 1975.

54 For the training of specialist temple officials and priests in the Old
Babylonian city of Ur and the importance of oral transmission at that
time, see Charpin 1986: 420–59.

55 For instance, in the Neo-Babylonian period arose a new post, that of
the *sepiru*, the scribe interpreter, who wrote on parchment or papyrus
in Aramaic – see Dandamayev M.A. 'The Social Position of Neo-
Babylonian Scribes' in Klengel 1982: 42–68.

56 See Pearce L. 1993 'Statement of Purpose: Why the Scribes Wrote' in
Cohen, Snell and Weisberg 1993: 185–93.

57 See, for instance, the well-known scribe during the reign of Nabonidus
called Itti-Marduk-balatu, a descendant of the Egibi family, whose
career spanned some forty-three years. He also acted as an entrepre-
neur dealing with banking operations and money-lending – see
Dandamayev 1982 'Social Stratification in Babylon 17th–4th centuries
C.C.' in Klengel 1982 (Gesellschaft und Kultur im alten Vorderasien)
(Berlin): 433–44.

58 See Porter 1993.

59 Dalley 1989: 9.

60 'Advice to a Prince', line 1, Lambert 1960: 113.

61 See van Driel 2000: 8–9.

CHAPTER 4

1 Lines 135–47 from 'Counsels of Wisdom', probably from the Middle Babylonian period. Lambert 1960: 104–5.

2 Lines 21–2 Babylonian Theodicy, Lambert 1960: 70–1.

3 Kassite inscription on a cylinder seal, quoted by Lambert 1960: 231.

4 Oppenheim 1977: 171–4.

5 Ibid. 173.

6 See Lambert and Parker 1966 for the original text; for the translation only, Foster 1996: I, 350–401.

7 As in the flood-myth Atra-hasis for instance, or the *enuma elish*.

8 Called Belet-ili (Lady of the Gods) or Mamma, subsuming such goddesses as Ninhursaga, Nintu, Aruru, Dingirmah, Ba'u.

9 See Dalley 1989: 163–81.

10 See Lambert 1982.

11 See Leick 1994: 130–56, 232–46.

12 See C.J. Fuller 1984 *Servants of the Goddess* (Cambridge): 11f.

13 For instance, Lambert 1966. A notable exception are the 'divine love lyrics' that feature Marduk, Sarpanitum and Ishtar, see Lambert 1975.

14 For these problems see Margueron 1984: 23–35.

15 Various texts survive which detail offerings; these offerings contain primarily cereal-based food (made into bread, cakes, porridge and so on), meat, dairy products such as clarified butter, diverse fruit and condiments. See Chapter 5, 'Food and drink', and also Bottéro 1985.

16 Derived from Sumerian kisal.mah – kisal is usually translated as court, but could also be an ante-chamber or forecourt. On the ambiguity of Mesopotamian architectural terminology, see Soden 1989.

17 In the temple of Ningal at Ur, for instance, archaeologists found broken fragments of the base of Hammurabi's stele, a column which may have been the one dedicated by Rim-Sin of Larsa.

18 See Lenzen 1955. If a temple was dedicated to two deities, a divine couple for instance, there would be two parallel chambers of equal size, linked by an axial passage. Cf. Ningal temple at the Gipar at Ur.

19 See Soden 1989: 208 for further discussion.

20 Charpin 1986: 251 ff.

21 The rota had to be meticulously organised by full-time temple administrators, see Charpin 1986: 262–9.

22 See the example of Mannum-meshu-lissir from Nippur, who bought prebends from impoverished 'old' families, see Stone and Owen 1991.

23 See McEwan 1981.

24 Ibid. p. 7.

25 Ibid. p. 67.

26 Ibid. p. 109 – he quotes 3 shekel of silver per day as the porter's allotment which contrasted with 312 shekel per day paid to an *erib bituti*

27 Smith S. 'The Babylonian Ritual for the Consecration and Induction of a Divine Statue' *Journal of the Royal Asiatic Society* 1925: 37–60.

28 Kingsbury 1963.

29 For instance, statues used to be washed and cleansed at the time when the moon was about to enter its new quarter. See Laessoe 1955.

30 See Wilson 1994: 94–5.

31 This also finds an echo in the preparation of altar and priest for the celebration of mass in the catholic and orthodox traditions.

32 See Charpin 1986: 378.

33 Borger 1973.

34 There are indications that most cult functionaries wore distinctive clothing to signal their rank and function but the few available descriptions still leave much to the imagination; the chief lamentation priest at Late Babylonian Uruk, for instance, was 'covered in a vestment of linen and bound to his head is a veil(?) to the lower part of his head' (McEwan 1981: 135).

35 Maul 1992: 159–71.

36 See, for instance, Ranke 1905 or Hölscher 1996.

37 So Oppenheim 1977: 183–98.

38 Tablet IV: 77–98, Lambert 1960: 61.

39 Woolley 1976.

40 The latter concept seems to have become prevalent as the source of suffering since the Middle Babylonian period.

41 See Ebeling 1931: 114 ff.

42 See Cunningham 1997: 177–9.

43 The nature of the disease gave some indication as to which deity could be involved; sexual dysfunction, for instance, could relatively easily be diagnosed as 'the hand of Ishtar' (the goddess of sexual life). See Mayer 1990 and Maul 1988.

44 So Cunningham 1997.

45 See Marwick M. (ed.) 1970 *Witchcraft and Sorcery* (Harmondsworth) for examples.

46 This was particularly the case in Assyria where upper-class women lived in close proximity in women's quarters – see Rollin 1987.

47 Col. I § 2, 'If a man brought a charge of witchcraft against another man but has not proved it, the one against whom the charge of witchcraft was made, upon going to the river (ordeal) shall throw himself into the river and if the river has then overpowered him, his accuser shall take his estate, if the river has shown that man to be innocent and accordingly he come out safe, the one who brought the charge of witchcraft against him shall be put to death, while the one who threw himself into the river shall take over the estate of his accuser'. It is not clear what constituted 'proof' but the river ordeal gave a fifty–fifty chance of being found guilty and hence the death penalty was meant to be an effective deterrent.

48 See, for instance, Abusch 1996.

49 Abusch 1990: 56.

50 See one performed by the famous *ašipu* Nabu-nadin-shumi for the Assyrian king Esarhaddon – in Parpola 1983: 203–4.

51 See Renger 1970.

52 See Gurney 1963 and Wiggermann 1992.

53 Wiggermann 1992: 125.

54 Ibid.

55 Sociologically ecstatic prophecy and spirit possession in the ancient Near East are linked to egalitarian societies which have undergone a political change towards stratification. The possessed are typically underprivileged or marginalised persons, often women, whose pronouncements uttered in the name of the deity serve to check abuse of power by the ruling elite – see Hoffmon H.B. 1992 'Prophecy: Ancient Near Eastern Prophecy' in Freedman D.N. (ed.) *Anchor Bible Dictionary* 5: 477–82; see also, for anthropological parallels, Obeyesekere G. 1981 *Medusa's Hair: An Essay on Personal Symbols and Religious Experience* (Chicago), and Crapanzano V. and V. Garrison (eds) 1977 *Case Studies of Spirit Possession* (New York). See also Uffenheimer B. 1999 *Early Prophecy in Israel* (translated from the Hebrew by David Louvish) (Jerusalem).

56 Oppenheim 1956.

57 See Veldhuis 1999; see also Larsen 1987.

58 See Friedman 1998.

59 Koch-Westenholz 1995.

60 Leichty 1969.

61 So Veldhuis 1999: 171–89.

62 E.g. 1958 *Symbolic Logic and the Game of Logic* (New York) or Foster J. 1973 *The Magic of Lewis Carroll* (Harmondsworth).

63 E.g. Wittgenstein L. 1953 *Philosophical Investigations* (London).

64 See Horton R. and R. Finnegan (eds) 1973 *Modes of Thought* (London).

65 Veldhuis 1999: 169.

66 For an anthropological analysis see Evans-Pritchard E.E. 1937 *Witchcraft, Oracles and Magic among the Azande* (Oxford).

67 In many royal inscriptions candidates for high office are described as having been 'chosen by the gods' or 'called by name to the office'.

68 See Finet 1966.

69 See Parpola 1983.

70 See Brown 2000.

71 Maul 1994.

72 Parpola 1970: no. 35.

73 See Parpola S. 'Mesopotamian Astrology and Astronomy as Domains of the Mesopotamian "Wisdom"', in Galter 1993: 54 f.

74 *Ludlul bel nemeqi* Tablet I, see Lambert 1960: 32–6.

75 A euphemism.

76 *Ludlul bel nemeqi* Tablet II, Lambert 1960 (tablet II): 43.

77 'Babylonian Theodicy', see Lambert 1960: 89.

CHAPTER 5

1 See Veenhof 1996.
2 See Margueron J.Cl. 'La Maison orientale' in Veenhof 1996: 17–38.
3 See ibid. p. 32. Margueron generally rejects the notion that the typical Mesopotamian house had a courtyard.
4 For the Old Babylonian period, see Y. Calvet 'Maisons privées paléo-babyloniennes à Larsa' in Veenhof 1996: 197–209; Stone 1987, Woolley 1976.
5 See Fathy H. 1986 *Natural Energy and Vernacular Architecture* (Chicago and London).
6 See Neumann H. 'Der sumerische Baumeister (šidim)' in Veenhof 1996: 153–69.
7 Lines 228–33, translation by T. Meek in Pritchard 1958: 139–40.
8 Heinrich and Seidl 1967.
9 At least no other similar elite tombs have yet been discovered.
10 Landsberger 1957: 154 ff.
11 See Leick 1994, plates 8–10.
12 See Simpson E. 'Furniture in Western Asia' in Sasson 1995, vol. III: 167; see generally also Salonen 1963.
13 See Reiter K. 'Haushaltsgegenstände in altbabylonischen Texten' in Veenhof 1996: 261–71.
14 Ibid. pp. 270–1.
15 Collon D. 'Clothing and Grooming in Ancient Western Asia' in Sasson 1995: 503–15.
16 He talks about 'wool bearing trees' being planted in the gardens of Nineveh.
17 Wright 1996; for a factory in Larsa employing more than 6000 workers, see Waetzold 1972.
18 Rouault 1977.
19 I, 196.
20 Museum of Aleppo, from Zimri-Lim's palace at Mari.
21 See T. Baqir 1946 *Iraq* 8: plate 12.
22 Vorderasiatisches Museum Berlin.
23 The picture of the Assyrian queen next to Ashurbanipal on a relief in the British Museum is unique.
24 Museum of Aleppo.
25 See the myth of Nergal and Ereshkigal, for instance, Dalley 1989: 170 f., col. iii; see also Leick 1994: 101.
26 Leick 1994: 42.
27 Old Babylonian version Tablet X, iii: Dalley 1989: 150.
28 VII, iii: Dalley 1989: 86–7.
29 Ebeling 1950.
30 'Precepts and admonitions', Lambert 1960: 102, lines 61–3.
31 Ellison 1981.
32 See Lambert 1960: 163, lines 22–9.

33 See Röllig 1970. For an ethno-archaeological experiment, see Katz and Maytag 1991.
34 A fever demon.
35 Tablet II SBViv, Dalley 1989: 24.
36 SBV II v Dalley 1989: 25–6.
37 Gibson 1992.
38 See Bottéro 1985.
39 Bottéro 1995.
40 Bottéro 1995: 17.
41 Bottéro 1995: 115 (B i 51–ii 20).
42 Lambert 1960: 247, 249 (my translation from the French).
43 See Parpola 1983.
44 Biggs 1967.
45 Biggs 1967: 33.
46 Ibid.
47 See Leick 1994, Plate 6–10.
48 Goodenick-Westenholz 1987.
49 See Black 1983.
50 See Lambert 1991: 152–3.
51 See l. 130, Code of Hammurabi.
52 Leick 1994: 180.
53 From Maqlu III, 1–12, see Leick 1994: 221.
54 As described in The Descent of Ishtar: when she disappears 'no young man made love to a girl in the street' (line 76).

BIBLIOGRAPHY

Abusch T. 1990 'An Early Form of the Witchcraft Ritual *maqlu* and the Origin of a Babylonian Magical Ceremony' in T. Abusch, J. Huehnergard and P. Steinkeller (eds) *Lingering over Words: Studies in Ancient Near Eastern Literature in Honor of William L. Moran* (Atlanta, Geo.) 1–57.

——1996 'Some Reflections on Mesopotamian Witchcraft' in A. Berlin (ed.) *Religion and Politics in the Ancient Near East* (Bethesda, Md.) 21–33.

Adams R. McC. 1981 *Heartland of Cities* (Chicago).

Algaze G. 1993 *The Uruk World System: The Dynamics of Expansion of Early Mesopotamian Civilization* (Chicago).

Aström P. (ed.) 1987–9 *High, Middle or Low? Acts of an International Colloquium on Absolute Chronology* 3 vols (Gothenburg).

Beaulieu P.-A. 1989 *The Reign of Nabonidus King of Babylon 556–539 BC* (New Haven, Conn.).

——1995 'King Nabonidus and the Neo-Babylonian Empire' in J.M. Sasson 1995: 969–80.

Berger P.R. 1973 *Die neubabylonischen Königsinschriften* (Neukirchen-Vluyn, Germany).

Biggs R.D. 1967 *ŠÀ.ZI.GA, Ancient Mesopotamian Potency Incantations* (Locust Valley, New York).

Black J.A. 1983 'Babylonian Ballads: A New Genre' *Journal of the American Oriental Society* 103:25–34.

Bongenaar A.C.V.M. (ed.) 2000 *Interdependency of Institutions and Private Entrepreneurs* (Leiden).

Bongenaar A.C.V.M. and B.J.J. Haring 1994 'Egyptians in Neo-Babylonian Sippar' *Journal of Cuneiform Studies* 46:59–72.

Borger R. 1965 'Der Aufstieg des neubabylonischen Reiches' *Journal of Cuneiform Studies* 19:59–78.

——1973 'Weihe eines Enlil Priesters' *Bibliotheca Mesopotamia* 30: 163–95.

Bottéro J. 1985 'The Cuisine of Ancient Mesopotamia' *Biblical Archaeology* 481:3047.

——1995 *Textes culinaires Mésopotamiens* (Winona Lake, Ind.).

Brinkman J.A. 1968 *A Political History of Post-Kassite Babylonia* (Rome).

Brown D. 2000 *Mesopotamian Planetary Astronomy–Astrology* (Groningen).

Buccellati G. 1966 *Amorites of the UrIII Period* (Naples).

Buringh P. 1957 'Living Conditions in the Lower Mesopotamian Plain in Ancient Times' *Sumer* 13:30–57.

Butzer K.W. 1995 'Environmental Change in the Near East and Human Impact on the Land' in J.M. Sasson 1995: 123–51.

Charles M. 1988 'Irrigation in Lowland Mesopotamia' *Bulletin on Sumerian Agriculture* 4: 1–39.

Charpin D. 1986 *Le Clergé d'Ur au siècle d'Hammurabi* (Geneva and Paris).

Charvát P. 2002 *Mesopotamia: Before History* (London and New York).

Cohen M.E., Snell D.C., Weisberg D.B. (eds) 1993 *The Tablet and the Scroll: Near Eastern Studies in Honor of William W. Hallo* (Bethesda, Md).

Cohen R. and R. Westbrook (eds) 2000 *Amarna Diplomacy: The Beginnings of International Relations* (Baltimore and London).

Cooper J.S. 1983 *The Curse of Agade* (Baltimore).

Cunningham G. 1997 *'Deliver Me from Evil'. Mesopotamian Incantations 2500–1500 BC* (Studia Pohl, Series Maior 17) (Rome).

Dalley S. 1989 *Myths from Mesopotamia* (Oxford and New York).

Dandamayev M. 1984 *Slavery in Babylonia (626–331 BC)* (translation) (Illinois).

——1988 'The Neo-Babylonian Society and Economy' *Cambridge Ancient History* 3/2: 252–75.

Dercksen J.G. 1996 *The Old Assyrian Copper Trade in Anatolia* (Nederlands Historisch–Archaeologisch Instituut te Istanbul).

——1999 *Trade and Finance in Ancient Mesopotamia* (Leiden).

Diakonoff I.M. 1965 *Structure of Society and State in Early Dynastic Sumer* (Malibu).

——1972 'Socio-Economic Classes in Babylonia and the Babylonian Concept of Social Stratification' in D.O. Edzard (ed.) *Gesellschaftsklassen im alten Zweistromland* (Munich) 41–52.

——1982 'The Structure of Near Eastern Society before the Middle of the 2nd Millennium BC' *Oikumene* (Budapest) 3:7–100.

Doty L.T. 1977 *Cuneiform Archives from Hellenistic Uruk* (Yale).

Driver G.R. 1976 *Semitic Writing* (rev. edn) (Oxford).

Ebeling E. 1931 *Tod und Leben nach den Vorstellungen der Babylonier* (Berlin and Leipzig).

——1950 *Parfümrezepte und kultische Texte aus Assur* (Sonderdruck aus Orientalia 17–19). (Rome).

Ellison R. 1981 'Diet in Mesopotamia: The Evidence of the Barley Ration Texts (c.3000–1400 BC)' *Iraq* 43:35–45.

Finet A. (ed.) 1966 *La Divination en Mésopotamie ancienne et dans les régions voisins.* XIVe Rencontre Assyriologique Internationale, Paris 1966 (Paris).

Folmer M.L. 1995 *The Aramaic Language in the Achaemenid Period: A Study of Linguistic Variation* (Louvain).

Foster B. 1996 *From Distant Days: Myths, Tales and Poetry of Ancient Mesopotamia* (Bethesda, Md).

Frayne, D.R. 1992 *The Early Dynastic List of Geographical Names* (American Oriental Society, New Haven, Conn.).

——1993 *Royal Inscriptions of Mesopotamia: The Sargonic and Gutian Periods* (Toronto).

Friedman S.M. 1998 *If a City Is Set on a Height* vol. I (Philadelphia).

Funk B. 1982 'Babylonien im 7. und 6. Jahrhundert' in H. Klengel (ed.) *Gesellschaft und Kultur im alten Vorderasien* (Berlin).

Galter H.D. (ed.) 1993 *Die Rolle der Astronomie in den Kulturen Mesopotamiens* (Beiträge zum 3. Grazer Morgenländischen Symposium, (23–7 September 1991) (Graz).

Gasche H., J. Armstrong and S.W. Cole 1998 *The Fall of Babylon* (Chicago).

Gelb I.J. 1979 'Household and Family in Early Mesopotamia' in E. Lipinski *State and Temple Economy in the Ancient Near East* vol. I (Louvain) 1–97.

Gesche P. 2000 *Schulunterricht in Babylonien im ersten Jahrtausend v. Chr.* (Münster).

Gibson McG. 1992 'Patterns of Occupation at Nippur' in Ellis M. deJong (ed.) *Nippur at the Centennial* Papers read at the 35th Rencontre Assyriologique Internationale Philadelphia 1988 (Philadelphia) 38–54.

Gibson McG. and R.D. Biggs (eds) 1987 *The Organization of Power: Aspects of Bureaucracy in the Ancient Near East* (Chicago).

Goodenick-Westenholz J. 1987 'A Forgotten Love Song' in F. Rochberg-Halton (ed.) *Language and History: Philological and Historical Studies Presented to E. Reiner* (New Haven, Conn.) 415–25.

Guinan A. 1997 'Auguries of Hegemony: The Sex Omens of Mesopotamia' *Gender and History* 9/3: 423–61.

Gurney O.R. 1963 *Babylonian Prophylactic Figures and Their Rituals* (London).

Hallo W.W. and W.K. Simpson 1998 *The Ancient Near East: A History* (2nd edn 1998, 1st edn 1968) (Forth Worth, etc.).

Harley J.B. and D. Woodward 1987 *The History of Cartography* vol. I (Chicago and London).

Harris R. 1961 'The Process of Secularization under Hammurapi' *Journal of Cuneiform Studies* 15:17–24.

Healey J.F. 1990 *The Early Alphabet* (London).

Heinrich E. and U. Seidl 1967 'Grundrisszeichnungen aus dem alten Orient' *Mitteilungen des Deutschen Orient-Gesellschaft zu Berlin* 98:24–45.

Hölscher M. 1996 *Die Personennamen der kassitischen Texte aus Nippur* (Münster).

Horowitz W. 1998 *Mesopotamian Cosmic Geography* (Winona Lake, Ind.).

Jacobsen Th. 1982 *Salinity and Irrigation Agriculture in Antiquity* (Malibu: Bibliotheca Mesopotamica 14).

Katz S.H. and F. Maytag 1991 'Brewing an Ancient Beer' *Archaeology* July/August 1991.

Kingsbury E.C. 1963 'A Seven Day Ritual in Old Babylonian Cult at Larsa' *Hebrew Union College Annual* 34:1–34.

Klengel H. 1982 *Gesellschaft und Kultur im alten Vorderasien* (Berlin).

Koch-Westenholz U. 1995 *Mesopotamian Astrology: An Introduction to Babylonian and Assyrian Celestial Divination* (Copenhagen).

Koldewey R. 1990 *Das wiedererstehende Babylon* (5th rev. edn) (Munich).

Kramer S.N. 1981 *History Begins at Sumer* (3rd edn) (Philadelphia).

Kramer S.N. and I. Bernhardt 1970 'Der Stadtplan von Nippur, der älteste Stadtplan der Welt' *Wissenschaftliche Zeitschrift: Gesellschafts- und Sprachwissenschaftliche Reihe* 19:727–30.

Kraus F.R. 1969 'Von altmesopotamischen Erbrecht' in J. Brugman et. al. (eds) *Essays on Oriental Laws of Succession* (Leiden) 1–17.

——1974 'Das altbabylonische Königstum' in P. Garelli (ed.) *Le Palais et la Royauté* XIX Rencontre Assyriologique Internationale, Paris, 29 June–2 July 1971 (Paris).

Krecher J. 1970 *Das Geschäftshaus Egibi in Babylonien in neu-babylonischer und achämenidischer Zeit* (Münster).

Kuhrt A. 1987 'Usurpation, Conquest and Ceremonial: From Babylon to Persia' in D. Cannadine and S. Price (eds) *Rituals of Royalty: Power and Ceremonial in Traditional Societies* (Cambridge) 20–55.

——1995 *The Ancient Near East, c.3000–330 BC* (London).

Laessoe J. 1955 *Studies on the Assyrian Ritual and Series bît rimki* (Copenhagen).

Lambert W.G 1960 *Babylonian Wisdom Literature* (Oxford).

——1965 'Nebuchadnezzar King of Justice' *Iraq* 27:11ff.

——1966 'Divine Love Lyrics' *Mitteilungen des Instituts für Orientforschung* 12:41–57.

——1971 'Nebuchadnezzar I: A Turning Point in the History of Mesopotamian Religion' in W.S. MacCullugh (ed.) *The Seed of Wisdom: Essays in Honor of T.G. Meek* (Toronto) 3–13.

——1975 'The Problem of the Love Lyrics' in H. Goedicke and J.J.M. Roberts (eds) *Unity in Diversity* (Baltimore) 98–135.

———1982 'The Hymn to the Queen of Nippur' in M. Stol, K.R. Veenhof and G. van Driel (eds) *Zikir šumim, Assyriological Studies Presented to F.R. Kraus* (Leiden) 173–218.

———1991 'Prostitution' in V. Haas (ed.), *Aussenseiter und Randgruppen* (Xenia: Konstanzer Althistorische Vorträge und Forschungen 32)(Konstanz) 127–57.

Lambert W.G. and B. Parker 1966 *Enuma eliš. The Babylonian Epic of Creation. The Cuneiform Text* (Oxford).

Landsberger B. 1957 *Materialien zum Sumerischen Lexikon* vol. V (Rome).

———1974 *The series HAR-ra=hubullu. Tablets XX–XXIV* (Materials for the Sumerian Lexikon xi) (Rome).

Larsen M.T. 1967 *Old Assyrian Caravan Procedures* (Istanbul).

———1987 'The Babylonian Lukewarm Mind: Reflections on Science, Divination, and Literacy' in E. Rochberg-Halton (ed.) *Language, Literature and History: Philological and Historical Studies Presented to Erica Reiner* (New Haven, Conn.) 203–25.

Leach E. 1976 *Culture and Communication: The Logic by which Symbols Are Known* (Cambridge).

Leemans W.F. 1950 *The Old Babylonian Merchant, His Business and Social Position* (Leiden: Studia et documenta ad iura Orientis Antiqui pertinetia III).

———1960 *Foreign Trade in the Old Babylonian Period as Revealed by Texts from Southern Mesopotamia* (Leiden: Studia et documenta ad iura Orientis Antiqui pertinetia VI).

Leichty E. 1969 *The Omen Series Šumma Izbu* (Glückstadt).

Leick G. 1994 *Sex and Eroticism in Mesopotamian Literature* (London and New York).

———2001 *Mesopotamia: The Invention of the City* (Harmondsworth).

Lenzen H. 1955 Mesopotamische Tempelanlagen von der Frühzeit bis zum zweiten Jahrhundert' *Zeitschrift für Assyriologie* 17:1–36.

Liverani M. (ed.) 1993 *Akkad: The First World Empire. Structure, Ideology, Traditions* (Padova).

McEwan G.J.P. 1981 *Priest and Temple in Hellenistic Babylonia* (Wiesbaden).

Margueron J.Cl. 1984 'Prolégomènes à une étude portant sur l'organisation de l'éspace sacré en Orient' in *Temples et sanctuaires, Seminaire de recherche 1981–1983 sous la direction de G. Roux* (Paris) 23–36.

Maul S.M. 1988 *Herzberuhigungsklagen: Die sumerisch-akkadischen Eršahunga Gebete* (Wiesbaden).

———1992 "kurgarru und assinnu und ihr Stand in der Babylonischen Gesellschaft' in V. Haas (ed.) *Aussenseiter und Randgruppen: Beiträge zu einer Sozialgeschichte des Alten Orient* (Xenia: Konstanzer Althistorische Vorträge und Forschungen 32) (Konstanz) 159–71.

——1994 *Zukunftsbewältigung. Eine Untersuchung altorientalischen Denkens anhand des babylonisch-assyrischen Lösungsrituals* (Mainz am Rhein).

Mayer W.P. 1990 '6 Šu-ila Gebete' *Orientalia, Nova series* 59:449–90.

Mieroop M. van de 1992 *Society and Enterprise in Old Babylonian Ur* (Berlin).

Milano L., S. de Martino, F.M. Fales, G.B. Lanfranchi (eds) 1999 *Landscapes, Territories, Frontiers and Horizons in the Ancient Near East.* Papers Presented to the XLIV Rencontre Assyriologique Internationale, Venice, 7–11 July 1997 (3 vols) (Padova).

Millard A.R. 1987 'Cartography in the Ancient Near East' in J.B. Harley and D. Woodward (eds) *The History of Cartography* (Chicago) 107–16.

Moran W.L. 1992 *The Amarna Letters* (Baltimore and London).

Moorey P.R.S. 1994 *Ancient Mesopotamian Materials and Industries: The Archaeological Evidence* (Oxford).

Neuman J. and S. Parpola 1987 'Climate Change and the 11th–10th Century Eclipse of Assyria and Babylonia' *Journal of Near Eastern Studies* 46:161–82.

Nissen H. 1988 *The Early History of the Ancient Near East 9000–2000 BC* (Chicago and London).

Nissen H., P. Damerow and R. Englund 1993 *Archaic Book-keeping: Early Writing and Techniques of Economic Administration in the Ancient Near East* (translated by P. Larsen) (Chicago).

Oppenheim A.L. 1956 *The Interpretation of Dreams in the Ancient Near East: With a Translation of the Assyrian Dream Book* (Philadelphia, PA).

——1967 'A New Look at the Structure of Mesopotamian Society' *Journal of the Economic and Social History of the Orient* 10:1–15.

——1977 *Ancient Mesopotamia: Portrait of a Dead Civilization* (2nd edn) (Chicago).

Parpola S. 1970/1983 *Letters from Babylonian and Assyrian Scholars to Kings Esarhaddon and Aššurbanipal* 2 parts (Neukirchen-Vluyn, Germany).

Pearce L. 1993 'Statement of Purpose: Why the Scribes Wrote' in M.E. Cohen, D.C. Snell, D.B. Weisberg (eds) *The Tablet and the Scroll: Near Eastern Studies in Honor of William W. Hallo* (Bethesda, Md) 185–93.

Pollock S. 1999 *Ancient Mesopotamia* (Cambridge).

Polyani K., C.M. Arensberg and H.W. Pearson (eds) 1957 *Trade and Markets in Early Empires* (Chicago).

Porter B.N. 1993 *Images Power and Politics* (Memoirs of the American Philosophical Society 208).

Postgate J.N. 1992 *Early Mesopotamia: Society and Economy at the Dawn of History* (London).

Pritchard J.B. 1958 *The Ancient Near East: An Anthology of Texts and Pictures* (Princeton).

Ranke H. 1905 *Early Babylonian Personal Names* (Philadelphia).

Reisman D. 1973 'Iddin-Dagan's Sacred Marriage Hymn' *Journal of Cuneiform Studies* 25:189–202.

Renger J. 1970 'Untersuchungen zum Priestertum in der altbabylonischen Zeit' *Zeitschrift für Assyriologie* N.S. 25:223–7.

Röllig W. 1970 *Das Bier im alten Mesopotamien* (Berlin).

Rollin S. 1987 'Women and Witchcraft in Ancient Assyria' in A. Cameron and A. Kuhrt (eds) *Images of Women in Antiquity* (London and Sydney) 34–46.

Rouault O. 1977 *Mukannišum: L'administration et l'économie palatiale à Mari* (Paris).

Sack R.H. 1983 'The Nabonidus Legend' *Révue d'Assyriologie* 77:67–131.

Salonen A. 1963 *Die Möbel des alten Mesopotamiens nach sumerisch-akkadischen Quellen* (Helsinki).

Sanlaville P. 1989 'Considerations sur l'évolution de la Basse Mésopotamie au cours des dernières millénaires' *Paléorient* 15 (2):5–27.

Sasson J.M. (ed.) 1995 *Civilizations of the Ancient Near East* (New York).

Schmandt-Besserat D. 1992 *Before Writing: From Counting to Cuneiform* (2 vols) (Austin).

Schwartz G. 1989 'The Origins of the Arameans in North Mesopotamia' in O.M.C. Haex, H.H. Curvers and P.M.M.G. Akkerman *To the Euphrates and Beyond: Archaeological Studies in Honour of Maurits N. van Loon* (Rotterdam) 275–91.

Sigrist M. 1984 *Les sattukku dans l' Ešumeša durant la période d'Isin et Larsa* (Malibu).

Sjöberg A.W. 1975 'The Old Babylonian Edubba', in St.J. Lieberman (ed.) *Sumerological Studies in Honor of Thorkild Jacobsen on his Seventieth Birthday June 7th 1974* (Chicago) 159–79.

Snell D.C. 1999 *Life in the Ancient Near East* (New Haven and London).

Soden W. von 1989 'Die Terminologie des Tempelbaus: Einleitung zum Colloquium am 6. Juni 1972' in L. Cagni and H.P. Müller (eds) *Wolfram von Soden: Aus Sprache, Geschichte und Religion Babyloniens. Gesammelte Aufsätze* (Naples) 203–13.

Stolper M.W. 1985 *Entrepreneurs and Empire: The Murašu Archive, the Murašu Firm and the Persian Rule in Babylonia* (Leiden).

Stone E.C. 1987 *Nippur Neighborhood* Studies in Ancient Oriental Civilizations 44 (Chicago).

Stone E.C. and Owen D.I. 1991 *Adoption in Old Babylonian Nippur and the Archive of Mannum-mešu-lissir* (Winona Lake, Ind.).

Tsukimoto A. 1985 *Untersuchungen zur Totenpflege (kispum) im alten Mesopotamien* (Neukirchen-Vluyn, Germany).

van Driel G. 2000 'Institutional and Non-Institutional Economy in Ancient Mesopotamia', in A.C.V.M. Bongenaar (ed.) *Interdependence of Institutions and Private Entrepreneurs* (Leiden) 22–3.

Veenhof K.R. (ed.) 1996 *Houses and Households in Ancient Mesopotamia* Papers Read at the 40ᵉ Rencontre Assyriologique Internationale, Leiden, 5–8 July 1993 (Istanbul and Leiden).

Veldhuis N. 1999 'Reading the Signs' in H.L.J. Vanstiphout et al. (eds) *All These Nations: Cultural Encounters within and with the Near East* (Groningen) 161–74.

Waetzold H. 1972 *Untersuchungen zur neusumerischen Textilindustrie* (Rome).

Walker C.B.F. 1987 *Cuneiform* (London).

Weiss H.P. 1986 *The Origins of Cities in Dry-Farming Syria and Mesopotamia in the Third Millennium BC* (Connecticut).

Wiggermann F.A.M. 1992 *Mesopotamian Protective Spirits: The Ritual Texts* (Groningen).

Wilson E.J. 1994 *'Holiness' and 'Purity' in Mesopotamia* (AOAT 237) (Neukirchen-Vluyn, Germany).

Woolley Sir L. 1954 *Excavations at Ur* (London).

——1976 *Ur Excavations* VII: *The Old Babylonian Period* (London).

Wright R.P. 1996 'Technology, Gender, and Class: Worlds of Difference in Ur III Mesopotamia' in R.P. Wright (ed.) *Gender and Archaeology* (Philadelphia: University of Pennsylvania Press) 79–110.

Wunsch C. 1993 *Die Urkunden des babylonischen Geschäftsmannes Iddin-Marduk: Zum Handel mit Naturalien* (Groningen).

Zettler R.L. 1992 '12th Century BC Babylonia: Continuity and Change' in W.A. Ward and M. Sharp Jonkowsky (eds) *The Crisis Years: The 12th Century BC* (Dubuque, Iowa) 174–81.

INDEX

Sumerian and Akkadian words